Phenomenological
Research
Methods

D0075083

Phenomenological Research Methods

WITHDRAWN

Clark Moustakas

SAGE Publications
International Educational and Professional Publisher
Thousand Oaks   London   New Delhi

Copyright © 1994 by Sage Publications, Inc.

For information address:

SAGE Publications, Inc.
2455 Teller Road
Thousand Oaks, California 91320
E-mail: order@sagepub.com

SAGE Publications Ltd.
6 Bonhill Street
London EC2A 4PU
United Kingdom

SAGE Publications India Pvt. Ltd.
M-32 Market
Greater Kailash I
New Delhi 110 048 India

Printed in the United States of America

Moustakas, Clark E.
    Phenomenological research methods / Clark Moustakas.
        p. cm.
    Includes bibliographical references and index.
    ISBN 0-8039-5798-X.—ISBN 0-8039-5799-8 (pbk.)
    1. Phenomenological psychology. 2. Psychology—Research—
Methodology. I. Title.
BF204.5. M68 1994
150.19'2—dc20   94-7355

03   04   10   9

Sage Production Editor: Astrid Virding

I dedicate Phenomenological Research Methods *to the learners and graduates of the Center for Humanistic Studies and The Graduate School of The Union Institute. From their investigations and my interactions with them, I have deepened and extended my knowledge of a wide range of human experiences and as an outcome have become a wiser, more effective teacher-guide and researcher.*

CONTENTS

ACKNOWLEDGMENTS

In the course of creating *Phenomenological Research Methods,* I have been significantly influenced by the English published works of Edmund Husserl and by his students and other phenomenological thinkers who clarified, expanded, and applied his ideas. Throughout this book, these authors and publishers are cited and appropriately credited.

I want to recognize the following persons from whose work I have borrowed relevant phenomenological theories, concepts, and methods, as well as examples of phenomenological data: C. M. Aanstoos, R. B. Addison, N. Alpern, J. Becker, F. M. Buckley, P. R. Colaizzi, R. Copen, H. Cooper, A. J. J. de Koning, C. T. Fischer, W. F. Fischer, C. B. Fraelich, A. Giorgi, E. Humphrey, E. Keen, K. LaCourse, J. Miesel, S. Palaian, C. Palmieri, P. Paskiewicz, M. Patton, C. Rhodes, L. Schmidt, E. Schneider, E. L. Stevick, C. Stratman, M. Trumbull, A. van Kaam, J. Van Maanen, R. von Eckartsberg, F. J. Wertz, D. R. Wolf, and P. Yoder.

I also thank the following authors and publishers for permission to use extended quotations from their works. Credit (following exerpted quotations) for permission to reprint material from the following or any other sources includes as well all quotations from that particular work used throughout this book.

N. Alpern. (1984). Men and Menstruation: A Phenomenological Investigation of Men's Experience of Menstruation. (Doctoral dissertation, Union for Experimenting Colleges and Universities, 1983). *Dissertation Abstracts International, 44,* 2883B.

R. Copen. (1993). Insomnia: A Phenomenological Investigation. (Doctoral dissertation, The Union Institute, 1992). *Dissertation Abstracts International, 53,* 6542B.

A. J. J. de Koning. (1979). "The Qualitative Method of Research in the Phenomenology of Suspicion." In A. Giorgi, R. Knowles, & D. L. Smith (Eds.), *Duquesne Studies in Phenomenological Psychology* (Vol. 3). Pittsburgh: Duquesne University Press.

W. F. Fischer. (1989). "An Empirical-Phenomenological Investigation of Being Anxious." In R. S. Valle & S. Halling (Eds.), *Existential-Phenomenological Perspectives in Psychology.* New York: Plenum.

C. B. Fraelich. (1989). A Phenomenological Investigation of the Psychotherapist's Experience of Presence. (Doctoral dissertation, The Union Institute, 1988). *Dissertation Abstracts International, 50,* 1643B.

A. Giorgi. (Ed.). (1985). *Phenomenology and Psychological Research.* Pittsburgh: Duquesne University Press.

E. Humphrey. (1991). Searching for Life's Meaning: A Phenomenological and Heuristic Exploration of the Experience of Searching for Meaning in Life. (Doctoral dissertation, The Union Institute, 1992). *Dissertation Abstracts International, 51,* 4051B.

E. Husserl. (1931). *Ideas* (W. R. Boyce Gibson, Trans.). London: George Allen & Unwin.

E. Keen. (1984). "Emerging From Depression." *American Behavioral Scientist, 27*(6), 801-812.

J. A. Miesel. (1991). A Phenomenological Exploration of the Experience of Voluntarily Changing One's Career During Midlife. (Doctoral dissertation, The Union Institute, 1991). *Dissertation Abstracts International, 52,* 5542B.

S. Palaian. (1993). The Experience of Longing: A Phenomenological Investigation. (Doctoral dissertation, The Union Institute, 1993). *Dissertation Abstracts International, 54,* 1678B.

C. Palmieri. (1990). The Experience of Adults Abused as Children. (Doctoral dissertation, The Union Institute, 1990). *Dissertation Abstracts International, 51,* 2631B.

P. Paskiewicz. (1988). The Experience of a Traumatic Closed Head Injury: A Phenomenological Study. (Doctoral dissertation, Union for Experimenting Colleges and Universities, 1987). *Dissertation Abstracts International, 49,* 919B.

C. Rhodes. (1987). Women in Transition: From Dependency to Autonomy: A Study in Self Development. (Doctoral dissertation, The Union Graduate School, 1986). *Dissertation Abstracts International, 48,* 572B.

E. Schneider. (1987). The Mother's Experience of the Mother-Daughter Relationship During the Daughter's Adolescent Years. (Doctoral dissertation, The Union Graduate School, 1986). *Dissertation Abstracts International, 48,* 2109B.

C. Stratman. (1990). The Experience of Personal Power for Women. (Doctoral dissertation, The Union Institute, 1989). *Dissertation Abstracts International, 50,* 5896B.

A. Strauss & J. Corbin. (1990). *Basics of Qualitative Research: Grounded Theory, Procedures, and Techniques.* Newbury Park, CA: Sage.

M. Trumbull. (1993). The Experience of Undergoing Coronary Artery Bypass Surgery: A Phenomenological Investigation. (Doctoral dissertation, The Union Institute, 1993). *Dissertation Abstracts International, 54,* 1115B.

P. Yoder. (1990). Guilt, the Feeling and the Force: A Phenomenological Study of the Experience of Feeling Guilty. (Doctoral dissertation, The Union Institute, 1989). *Dissertation Abstracts International, 50,* 5341B.

I express my appreciation to Helen Saxton for typing sections of the revised manuscript and especially Vange Puszcz who put the entire manuscript on a computer, corrected all errors, followed up on missing reference data, and in countless other ways made possible the completion of this book project, and Jill Benton for library detective work.

I also express my gratitude to Kevin MacNeil who originated the idea and facilitated the process of publishing a work on my approach to phenomenological research.

FOREWORD

In developing *Phenomenological Research Methods,* I have been inspired and to some degree guided by comments and questions of graduate students and research professors who had employed phenomenological models in their studies of a wide range of human behavior and experience. I have no doubt that our conversations and dialogues have made this book more useful as theory, concept, design, and method for human science inquiry. A brief summary outline of chapters follows.

Chapter 1, "Human Science Perspectives and Models," discusses and illustrates five human science research approaches that utilize qualitative methodologies. The models are Ethnography, Grounded Theory, Hermeneutics, Empirical Phenomenological Research, and Heuristic Research. The chapter includes a description of perspectives and qualities that these models hold in common. This opening chapter is also a way of distinguishing my own phenomenological model from that of other major human science guides to conducting research.

Chapter 2, "Transcendental Phenomenology: Conceptual Framework," presents a conceptual framework for understanding Transcendental Phenomenology and the theoretical and methodological bases for the development of the phenomenological model that guides my approach to human science inquiry.

Chapter 3, "Phenomenology and Human Science Inquiry," offers further delineations of traditional empirical science and human science. The chapter includes discussions of the core concepts—consciousness, act, perception, intentional experience, and intersubjective validity. An illustration of the application of phenomenological theory and method to education is included.

Chapter 4, "Intentionality, Noema, and Noesis," details the three major concepts of Husserl's transcendental phenomenology that guided my construction of a design for obtaining and collecting data that explicates themes, meanings, and essences of human experience.

Chapter 5, "Epoche, Phenomenological Reduction, Imaginative Variation, and Synthesis," presents the major processes that are followed in doing research phenomenologically.

Chapter 6, "Methods and Procedures for Conducting Human Science Research," enables the researcher to follow, step by step, the methods and procedures needed for preparation and collection of data, for conducting interviews, and for organizing and analyzing data into a unified and coherent portrayal of the experience investigated. The chapter offers examples of how to formulate a research question and locate and select research participants. It discusses relevant ethical standards for conducting research with human participants. The chapter illustrates how to conduct a review of the professional literature and suggests resources and strategies for developing a summary of relevant prior works. A comprehensive example is provided on organizing and developing the review of literature section of a research report.

Chapter 7, "Phenomenological Research: Analyses and Examples," presents two major designs and methods for organizing and analyzing data. Significant examples from recent investigations are included to illustrate Horizonalization, Invariant Horizons, Individual Textural Descriptions, Individual Structural Descriptions, Composite Textural and Composite Structural Descriptions, and the Synthesis of Meanings and Essences.

Chapter 8, "Summary, Implications, and Outcomes: A Phenomenological Analysis," illustrates entire phenomenological studies and provides examples of future research projects, and the personal, social, and professional implications of research.

An Appendix section is included offering examples of a letter of instructions to research participants, a participant release agreement, and a letter of appreciation. Also in the Appendix section is a detailed outline guide for conducting transcendental phenomenological research, and an outline to guide the creation of the research manuscript.

The process of creating *Phenomenological Research Methods* has been a journey of intensive work sessions that involved literature reviews of about 100 research publications, a wide range of relevant professional works focusing on phenomenology, and hours of reflective thinking. Throughout, I have engaged in dialogues with learners at the Center for Humanistic Studies in my courses "Foundations for Human Science Research" and "Human Science Research Designs," and with professors at the Center. I also have met often with my learners at the Graduate School of The Union Institute whose doctoral dissertations I supervise. Important too were self-dialogues that eventuated in searchings that moved from material references, resources, and data to internal wonderings, from thinking and reflecting to intuition and imagination, and from ideas to lingering images and visions.

I hope that *Phenomenological Research Methods* will provide practical guidance needed to conduct human science research and will inspire researchers and studies that will lead to significant new knowledge of everyday human experiences, human behavior, and human relationships.

※※※
1
※※※

HUMAN SCIENCE
PERSPECTIVES AND MODELS

In distinguishing my own phenomenological design and methodology from that of other qualitative models that guide human science research, of the various qualitative inquiries I will briefly outline five that stand out for me: Ethnography, Grounded Research Theory, Hermeneutics, Duquesne University's Phenomenology, and Heuristics. I will also list commonalities of theories of human science inquiry that guide qualitative research.

ETHNOGRAPHY

Ethnography involves extensive fieldwork and may be pursued in a variety of social settings that allow for direct observations of the activities of the group being studied, communications and interactions with the people, and opportunities for informal and formal interviews (Bogdan & Taylor, 1975; Jorgensen, 1989; Lofland, 1971). Ethnographic studies have been conducted from anthropological (Benedict, 1959; Mead, 1928, 1975), sociological (Van Maanen, Dabbs, & Faulkner, 1982) and psychological (DiGregorio, 1983; Holmes, 1993) perspectives or frameworks. Van Maanen (1982) observed that:

> The result of ethnographic inquiry is cultural description. It is, however, a description of the sort that can emerge only from a lengthy period of intimate study and residence in a given social setting. It calls for the language spoken in that setting, first-hand participation in some of the activities that take place there, and, most critically, a deep reliance on intensive work with a few informants drawn from the setting. (pp. 103-104)

Ethnographic research involves an initial engagement of exploring, planning, getting ready to conduct the study, including obtaining permissions for observation and participation, exploring the geography of the setting, and developing a plan for the scheduling of visits.

Bogdan and Taylor (1975) offer these strategies: (1) Look for key words in observing interactions and in recording comments of participants and staff; (2) Concentrate on opening and closing statements; (3) Soon after leaving the setting, make notes of all that can be remembered; (4) Don't talk to anyone until recording of field notes has been completed; (5) Diagram physical layout of setting; and (6) Outline specific acts, events, activities, and conversations (p. 63). Patton (1990) suggests the following:

1. Be descriptive in taking field notes.
2. Gather a variety of information from different perspectives.
3. Cross-validate and triangulate by gathering different kinds of data—observations, interviews, program documentation, recordings, and photographs—and using multiple methods.
4. Use quotations; represent program participants in their own terms. Capture participants' views of their experiences in their own words.
5. Select key informants wisely and use them carefully. Draw on the wisdom of their informed perspectives, but keep in mind that their perspectives are limited.
6. Be aware of and sensitive to the different stages of fieldwork.
   a. Build trust and rapport at the entry stage. Remember that the evaluator-observer is also being observed and evaluated.
   b. Stay alert and disciplined during the more routine, middle phase of fieldwork.

c. Focus on pulling together a useful synthesis as fieldwork draws to a close.

d. Be disciplined and conscientious in taking detailed field notes at all stages of fieldwork.

7. Be as involved as possible in experiencing the program as fully as possible while maintaining an analytical perspective grounded in the purpose of the fieldwork.

8. Clearly separate description from interpretation and judgment.

9. Provide formative feedback as part of the verification process of fieldwork. Time that feedback carefully. Observe its impact.

10. Include in your field notes and evaluation report your own experiences, thoughts, and feelings. These are also field data (pp. 273-274).

Wolf's study (1991) of motorcycle clubs is a fine example of ethnographic participant-observation research. In conducting his investigation he observed and participated in a range of activities that included drinking and socializing with the members; assisting them in the customizing or repairing of their motorcycles; loaning money to or borrowing money from them; exchanging motorcycle parts; engaging in conversations at a motorcycle shop; joining them on a duck hunt, fishing trips, and dinners; riding with them; and adding his physical presence when club members were being threatened. After 2 years of involvement with the bikers, Wolf's relationship with them became less frequent and less intense and ultimately ended entirely. He comments on his departure:

> What I shared with these men led me to believe that I would at least maintain ties of friendship after I completed the ethnography. The enduring emotion would be one of comradeship. I was wrong. I would be like so many of the ex-members who simply drifted away, never to be seen or spoken of again. (p. 222)

Patton (1990) has summarized the values of participant observation research: (1) By direct observation the researcher is better able to understand the context in which the people live and share activities and their lives; (2) First-hand experience enables the researcher to be open to discover and deduce what is significant; (3) The researcher is able directly to observe activities and infer meanings not in the awareness of participants and staff; (4) Through direct observation, the researcher can learn things that research participants and staff may not be willing to disclose; (5) The researcher can include his or her own perceptions of what is essential in understanding the setting, its participants and staff; and (6) First-hand observation and participation enables the researcher to gather data through direct experience and thus be able to understand and interpret the setting and participants being studied and evaluated.

GROUNDED RESEARCH THEORY

Another qualitative approach in human science inquiries is known as grounded theory. In this research approach, the focus initially is on unraveling the elements of experience. From a study of these elements and their interrelationships a theory is developed that enables the researcher to understand the nature and meaning of an experience for a particular group of people in a particular setting (Glaser & Strauss, 1967). In grounded research the theory is generated during the research process and from the data being collected. The hypotheses and concepts are worked out in the course of conducting the study and from an analysis of data.

In his book, *Qualitative Analysis for Social Scientists,* Strauss (1987) defines grounded theory as a detailed grounding of the research inquiry by careful analysis of the data, involving the examination of field notes, study of the transcribed interviews sentence by sentence, coding of each sentence or phrase, sorting the codes, making comparisons among the categories, and ultimately constructing a theory. During the process "the researcher puts down theoretical questions, hypotheses, summary of codes" thus "keeping track of coding results and stimulating further coding, and also a major means for integrating the theory" (p. 22). The

> procedures for discovering, verifying, and formulating grounded theory . . . are in operation all through the research project and . . . go on in close relationship to each other, in quick sequence and often simultaneously. . . . Memos are likely to become increasingly elaborate, summarizing the previous ones or focusing closely on closing gaps in the theory. (Strauss, 1987, pp. 23-24)

Although the ultimate aim is to construct an integrated theory, "no sequential steps are laid out in advance." Each research project has "its own detailed sequences" that depend on the data available, the interpretations and experience of the researcher, and the contingencies that influence and guide the research, both personally and professionally (p. 24).

Using grounded interpretative research in an investigation of physician socialization, Addison (1989) includes the following tenets and practices:

1. Grounded theory researchers continually question gaps in the data—omissions and inconsistencies, and incomplete understandings. They continually recognize the need for obtaining information on what influences and directs the situations and people being studied.
2. Grounded theory researchers stress open *processes* in conducting of research rather than fixed methods and procedures.
3. Grounded theorists recognize the importance of context and social structure.
4. Grounded theory researchers generate theory and data from interviewing processes rather than from observing individual practices.
5. In grounded theory research, data collecting, coding, and analysis occur simultaneously and in relation to each other rather than as separate components of a research design.
6. Grounded theory is an inductive process: theory must grow out of the data and be grounded in that data. (p. 41)

As grounded research is conducted, the experience being observed is labeled. Strauss and Corbin (1990) illustrate the process in the following:

Suppose you are in a fairly expensive but popular restaurant. . . . While waiting for your dinner, you notice a lady in red. She appears to be just standing there in the kitchen, but your common sense tells you that a restaurant wouldn't pay a lady in red just to stand there, especially in a busy kitchen. Your curiosity is piqued, so you decide to do an inductive analysis to see if you can determine just what her job is . . .

You notice that she is intently looking around the kitchen area, *a work site,* focusing here and then there, taking a mental note of what is going on. *You ask yourself, what is she doing here?* Then you label it *watching.* Watching what? *Kitchen work.*

Next, someone comes up and asks her a question. She answers. This act is different than watching, so *you code* it as *information passing.*

She seems to notice everything. You call this *attentiveness.* Our lady in red walks up to someone and tells him something. Since this incident also involves information that is passed on, you also label it, *information passing.* Although standing in the midst of all this activity, she doesn't seem to disrupt it. *To describe this phenomenon* you use the term *unintrusiveness.* She turns and walks quickly and quietly, *efficiency,* into the dining area, and proceeds to *watch,* the activity here also.

She seems to be keeping track of everyone and everything, *monitoring.* But monitoring what? Being an astute observer you notice that she is monitoring the *quality* of the service, how the waiter interacts and responds to the customer; the *timing of service,* how much transpires between seating a customer, their ordering, the delivery of food; and *customer response and satisfaction* with the service.

A waiter comes with an order for a large party, she moves in to help him, *providing assistance.*

The woman looks like she knows what she is doing and is competent at it, *experienced.*

She walks over to a wall near the kitchen and looks at what appears to be a schedule, *information gathering.*

The maitre d' comes down and they talk for a few moments and look around the room for empty tables and judge at what point in the meal the seated customers seem to be: the two are *conferring.* (pp. 63-64)

I have selected Montgomery's (1990, 1991) study of the care-giving relationship to illustrate grounded theory research. Her study focused on understanding caring from the perspective of the care-giver's experience. Montgomery herself worked with nurses as a psychiatric/mental health consultant in hospital settings. She states: "I used a naturalistic grounded theory approach in which I interviewed nurses and asked them to talk about experiences that stood out for them" (1991, p. 92). The 35 nurses who were interviewed had been referred to Montgomery by others who believed that these nurses were "exemplars of caring." From the interviewing and the data, the "over-riding theme of caring was the experience of spiritual transcendence . . . defined as experiencing oneself in relation to a force greater than oneself" (p. 92). The spiritual dimension included three properties: (1) Caring is a spiritually transcendent phenomenon distinguished from "over-involvement, rescuing or co-dependency." (2) Caring awakens a source of energy that accounts for "how spiritual transcendence serves as an important resource for self renewal and motivation for the care-giver, so that caring is associated with profound fulfillment and growth rather than burnout." (3) Caring, inspired by spiritual transcendence, provides the care-giver with a sense of personal fulfillment and emotional satisfaction (p. 93). An example of the spiritual dimension is exemplified by the following narrative of one of the care-givers in Montgomery's research:

> Spiritualness . . . comes from a deep sense of ministration to the individual. You minister to the spirit within the body. Sometimes you will not even recognize the person outwardly because of deterioration. You minister to the spirit. . . . I wasn't aware of that twenty-years ago, and I think for many nurses it's dormant. (Montgomery, 1991, p. 97)

Another care-giver contributes this portrayal of the spiritual dimension: "There is an endless amount of love of God for people. . . . God has given to the whole, to everybody, and it's available to be used. And so I can love these people with my whole heart" (p. 103).

In a concluding comment on her grounded theory research, Montgomery (1991) emphasizes that care-givers draw upon spiritual energy and courage in the process of helping people heal their physical, emotional, and psychological pain. Care-giving "becomes a self-enhancing way of being" such that the care-giver experiences the essential truth of care-giving, that it comes from the heart, and that "helping to heal them heals our hearts as well" (p. 103).

In closing, I refer to Strauss's (1987) comments on grounded theory research: "The grounded theory of analysis . . . involves a grounding in data. Scientific theories require first of all that they be conceived, then elaborated, then checked out." The aspects of inquiry are induction, deduction, and verification. "Consider induction first: Where do the insights, hunches, generative questions come from? Answer: They come from experience . . . from actual exploratory research into the phenomenon, or from a previous research program, or from theoretical sensitivity" derived from the knowledge of the technical literature. "As for deduction: Success at it rests . . . on the ability to think logically" and "with experience about the particular kind of data under scrutiny. . . . And verification. . . . It involves knowledge about sites, events, actions, actors, also procedures and techniques (and learned skills in thinking about them)" (pp. 12-13).

HERMENEUTICS

The focus on consciousness and experience, essential in ethnographic, participant-observation, and grounded theory research, is also a central emphasis in hermeneutics. In his introduction to the human studies, Dilthey (1976) asserts that,

> all science and scholarship is empirical but all experience is originally connected, and given validity, by our consciousness . . . it is impossible to go beyond consciousness, to see, as it were, without eyes or to direct a cognitive gaze behind the eye itself. . . . From this point of view our picture of the whole of nature stands revealed as a shadow cast by a hidden reality; undistorted reality exists for us in the facts of consciousness given by inner experience. (p. 161)

He adds: "To the perceiving mind the external world remains only a phenomenon but to the whole human being who wills, feels, and imagines" (p. 162) the external reality is immediately given and as certain as one's own self. "We do not know of this external world through an inference from effects to causes . . . cause and effect are only abstractions" (p. 162) from life. Thus, the horizon of experience widens: at first it only seems to tell us about our own inner states but in knowing oneself one also comes to know about the external world and other people (p. 162).

Makkreel (1975), referring to Schliermacher's meaning, comments that

> Hermeneutics must have more than a negative goal of overcoming obstacles in the way of regaining the original intention of the author. It must also allow for the more productive critique of a work whereby the particular intentions of the author can be refined, either by uncovering what fundamentally underlies them or going beyond them. (p. 267)

Dilthey (1976) accepted Schliermacher's general outline of hermeneutics, but added that a historical perspective is necessary "to the hermeneutic task of understanding an author better than" the author understands his or her own experience (p. 267).

Dilthey (1976) believed that to understand human experience, in addition to description of the experience as such, it was necessary to study history and that studies of experience are dependent on historical groundings and on descriptions in order to form a whole. He emphasized that, "We must discover how human studies are related to the fact of humanity . . . chemical effects of gunpowder (for example) are as much a part of the course of modern war as the moral qualities of the soldiers who stand in its smoke" (p. 172). History adds to the meaning of experience by reflecting on political and economic activities, settlements, and wars.

> They fill our souls with great images about the historical world which surrounds us: but what moves us, above all, in these accounts is what is inaccessible to the senses and can only be experienced inwardly; this is inherent in the outer events which originate from it and, in turn, is affected by them. (Dilthey, 1976, p. 172)

Thus, hermeneutic science involves the art of reading a text so that the intention and meaning behind appearances are fully understood. There is a relationship, for example, "between a poetically sensitive listener's comprehension of a play and the most excellent literary-historical analysis" (Dilthey, 1976, p. 182). This interrelationship—the direct conscious description of experience and the underlying dynamics or structures that account for the experience—provides a central meaning and unity that enables one to understand the substance and essence of the experience. Interrelationship of science, art, and history is at the heart of hermeneutic design and methodology.

In his hermeneutics of suspicion, Gadamer (1984), quoting Schliermacher, defines hermeneutics

> as the ability to avoid misunderstanding, because, as a matter of fact, that *is* the mystery of individuality. We can never be sure, and we have no proofs, of rightly understanding the individual utterance of another. However, even in the romantic era when this feeling for the individuality and the "closeness" of the individual became widespread, it was never doubted that *behind* a person's individuality something common and intelligible could be reenacted. (p. 57)

Hermeneutic analysis is required in order to derive a correct understanding of a text. "There are no moral phenomena," exclaims Nietzsche, "only moral interpretations of the phenomena" (Gadamer, 1984, p. 58). Gadamer adds, "it is no longer the manifest meaning of a statement of a text, but the text's and its interpreter's function in the preservation of life" (p. 58). Interpretation unmasks what is hidden behind the objective phenomena. Gadamer reinforces Heidegger's emphasis on hermeneutics showing that interpretation is not an isolated activity but the basic structure of experience (p. 58).

The hermeneutic process involves a circle through which scientific understanding occurs, through which we correct our prejudices or set them aside and hear "what the text says to us" (Gadamer, 1976, p. xviii). In the hermeneutic circle, our prejudgments are corrected in view of the text, the understanding of which leads to new prejudgments. The prejudgments that lead to preunderstanding are "constantly at stake;" their surrender could also be called a transformation. In the "process of being instructed" new preunderstandings are ceaselessly being formed (Gadamer, 1976, p. 38).

The text, or interview protocol, provides an important description of conscious experience. Reflective interpretation of the text is needed to achieve a fuller, more meaningful understanding, to bring "before me something that otherwise happens 'behind my back' " (Gadamer, 1976, p. xviii). The reflective-interpretative process includes not only a description of the experience as it appears in consciousness but also an analysis and astute interpretation of the underlying conditions, historically and aesthetically, that account for the experience. "Our possession by language is the ontological condition for our understanding of the texts that address us" (p. xxix).

For Gadamer, the starting points of hermeneutic studies are to be found in art and in philological-historical insights. Gadamer believes that "the autonomy of viewing art from the vantage point of the history of style has been shaken by hermeneutical reflection (1) on the concept of art itself, and (2) on concepts of individual styles and epochs . . . including shake up of fixed presuppositions" which then make scientific progress and new questions possible (1976, pp. 38-39).

The editors of the *Duquesne Studies in Phenomenological Psychology* (Volume 3, 1979), A. Giorgi, R. Knowles, and D. L. Smith, adopt a hermeneutical-phenomenological psychology, stating:

Up to now, empirical-phenomenological psychology proceeded by collecting protocols descriptive of the subjects' experience (e.g. learning, envy, anxiety, etc.), and then systematically and rigorously interrogating these descriptions step by step to arrive at the structure of the experience. Hermeneutical psychology suggests another data source and a different method of analysis. (p. 179)

The protocols "call for interpretation analogous to the interpretation of a text" (p. 180). The process of analysis involves Ricoeur's four criteria: " 1) a fixation on meaning, 2) dissociation at some point from the mental intention of the subject (author), 3) the necessity to interpret the protocols (texts) as a whole, a gestalt of interconnected meanings, 4) their universal range of address, i.e., their potentiality for multiple interpretations" (p. 180). Thus, "the hermeneutical task is to find justifiable modes through which my experience and comprehension of the phenomenon being researched can serve as a bridge or access for elucidating and interpreting the meaning of the phenomenon" (Titelman, 1979, p. 188).

Jager's study (see Jager, 1979) of the worlds of festive celebration and mundane labor illustrates the enrichment of empirical phenomenology by the hermeneutical method. Jager returned to ancient myths of the Greek god Dionysus in analyzing the elements that comprise a myth. The editors observed that Jager

> leads us on a journey of description and reflection, revealing as he proceeds, various faces of the worlds of celebration and labor. Within the context of the Dionysian myths, he teases out and unpacks the meaning of human experience dwelling in the path and the abyss, the ivy and the fig, the wine, the wine and the grave. (Giorgi et al., 1979, p. 180)

Included in Jager's study is description and reflection, the essential components of empirical-phenomenological psychology, "but the creative interpretive act is primary" (Giorgi et al., 1979, p. 180).

Titelman (1979) adds: "The descriptive protocol, like the text, is an 'open-work' that awaits fresh interpretations from different personal perspectives and as history, in its unfolding, sheds new light on the experiences and events that have been described" (p. 186).

EMPIRICAL PHENOMENOLOGICAL RESEARCH

Perhaps the most frequent applications of phenomenological research as well as the development of theory, concepts, and processes involved in human science inquiry come from the *Duquesne Studies in Phenomenological Psychology,* Volumes 1 (Giorgi, Fischer, & von Eckartsberg, 1971), 2 (Giorgi, Fischer, & Murray, 1975), 3 (Giorgi et al., 1979), and

4 (Giorgi, Barton, & Maes, 1983). Van Kaam (1959, 1966) operation-
alized empirical phenomenological research in psychology. He investigated the experience of really feeling understood. Van Kaam (1966)
asked high school and college students to recall a situation or situations
in which they felt understood by someone, such as, one's mother, father,
girlfriend, or boyfriend. His emphasis was on obtaining descriptions of
their feelings. From an analysis of 80 of the 365 descriptions, he derived
the following constituents of "really feeling understood."

> Perceiving signs of understanding from a person; perceiving that a person
> co-experiences what things mean to subject; perceiving that the person
> accepts the subject; feeling satisfaction; feeling initially relief from expe-
> riential loneliness; feeling safe in the relationship with the person under-
> standing; feeling safe experiential communion with the person understanding;
> feeling safe experiential communion with that which the person under-
> standing is perceived to represent. (van Kaam, 1966, p. 325)

From his analysis of the descriptions, van Kaam (1966) derived a
general description of really feeling understood.

> The experience of "really feeling understood" is a perceptual-emotional Ge-
> stalt: A subject, perceiving that a person co-experiences what things mean to
> the subject and accepts him, feels, initially, relief from experiential loneliness,
> and, gradually, safe experiential communion with that person and with that
> which the subject perceives this person to represent. (pp. 325-326)

Van Kaam (1966) believes that a preconceived, experimental design
imposed on the "subjects" of an experiment, and statistical methods,
"may distort rather than disclose a given behavior through an imposition
of restricted theoretical constructs on the full meaning and richness of
human behavior" (p. 14). He emphasizes that:

> I can open myself to the phenomena themselves in either a critical or an
> uncritical way. The critical method of observation implies the use of the
> phenomenological method. This method leads, ideally, to the type of
> description and classification of phenomena which can be affirmed by
> experts in the same field of psychology. Research performed in this way
> is pre-empirical, pre-experimental, and pre-statistical; it is experiential and
> qualitative. It sets the stage for more accurate empirical investigations by
> lessening the risk of a premature selection of methods and categories; it is

object-centered rather than method-centered. Such preliminary exploration does not supplant but complements the traditional methods of research available to me. (van Kaam, 1966, p. 295)

The empirical phenomenological approach involves a return to experience in order to obtain comprehensive descriptions that provide the basis for a reflective structural analysis that portrays the essences of the experience. The approach "seeks to disclose and elucidate the phenomena of behavior as they manifest themselves in their perceived immediacy" (van Kaam, 1966, p. 15). The human scientist determines the underlying structures of an experience by interpreting the originally given descriptions of the situation in which the experience occurs.

Giorgi (1985) outlines two descriptive levels of the empirical phenomenological approach: Level I, the original data is comprised of naive descriptions obtained through open-ended questions and dialogue. On Level II, the researcher describes the structures of the experience based on reflective analysis and interpretation of the research participant's account or story (p. 69).

In Giorgi's terms,

by adopting a strictly descriptive approach, we can let the phenomena speak for themselves, and when we do we discover that whatever appears suggests in its very appearance something more which does not appear, which is concealed . . . the given that is in the appearance of phenomena is "directionality," a direction is offered or a significance is held out which we pick up and follow, or turn away from. (p. 151) [This and other quotes from this work are reprinted by permission of Duquesne University Press.]

The aim is to determine what an experience means for the persons who have had the experience and are able to provide a comprehensive description of it. From the individual descriptions general or universal meanings are derived, in other words the essences or structures of the experience.

Giorgi (1979) summarizes the methods of analysis as follows:

(1) The researcher reads the entire description of the learning situation straight through to get a sense of the whole. (2) Next, the researcher reads the same description more slowly and delineates each time that a transition in meaning is perceived with respect to the intention of discovering the meaning. (p. 83)

From this procedure, the researcher obtains

> a series of meaning units or constituents. (3) The researcher then eliminates redundancies and clarifies or elaborates to himself the meaning of the units he just constituted by relating them to each other and to the sense of the whole. (4) The researcher reflects on the given units, still expressed essentially in the concrete language of the subject, and comes up with the essence of that situation for the subject. Each unit is systematically interrogated for what it reveals. The researcher transforms each unit, when relevant, into the language of psychological science. (5) The researcher synthesizes and integrates the insights achieved into a consistent description of the structure of learning. (p. 83)

The understanding of meaningful concrete relations implicit in the original description of experience *in the context of a particular situation* is the primary target of phenomenological knowledge.

Giorgi (1985) illustrates the empirical phenomenological model with the following Naive and General Descriptions of the Situated Structures *of learning.* The concrete narrative of one co-researcher in Giorgi's study describes the experience of learning to drive.

Naive Description

Learning to drive was important to me at 16 because it meant I no longer needed to depend on others for transportation. So I was excited when my learner's permit came. My first time behind the wheel of the car was on a Sunday in an empty shopping center parking lot. I first learned how to start the car, what the PRNDL stood for, and where the emergency brake was. I practiced starting the car about five times and started to feel a little more confident even though the car still seemed huge.

Now I was ready to start to drive. I was nervous again and started to think maybe I wasn't ready to drive, maybe I should practice starting the car some more, as I was confident in doing that. But my teacher assured me I was ready. So I started the car, took the emergency brake off and the car moved a few feet. I remember thinking, "It's moving, it's moving" and then feeling really afraid because I was in control of the car and didn't really know what I was doing. The car moved a few feet and then I put the brakes on. They seemed really tight and jerked both of us forward. I felt I would never be able to put them on smoothly. But after driving a few feet and stopping, I felt a little more confident.

The next step was to take the car on the road. This was the most frightening time for me. The car seemed like a giant boat. I had visions of it going out of control or of my crashing into another car. As I went on to the road and in with traffic, I felt that my car was all over the road—that I took up all four lanes. Everyone seemed to be passing me—I seemed to be going slower than everyone else—but if I went faster, I was afraid the car would go out of control. The car also didn't seem to keep straight. I had to keep moving the wheel to keep it straight. When it was time for me to change lanes to pass other cars, I was always afraid that they would come into my lane and hit me or that I wouldn't be able to get back into the other lane. The car just seemed so big I didn't feel in control of it.

After learning to drive—and more important just driving—the car did not seem so big, and I could see it was no different from the other cars on the road. I also began to realize that the car stayed pretty straight without my turning the wheel all the time and that when I passed other drivers, they would stay in their lanes.

I viewed my car in the right perspective as compared to road size and other cars. (Giorgi, 1985, pp. 60-61)

General Description of Situated Structures of Learning

Learning is the awareness of the necessity to reorganize a personal project based upon the discrepancy between the implicit assumptions brought to a situation vital for the continuance of the project and the perception and understanding of the actions of others in terms of the project in the same situation. It is also manifested in S's discovery of the fact that he is prereflectively and ambiguously living out two conflicting roles with respect to the others involved in the project and in the ability of S to circumvent the difficulty by imagining he can choose to live out the project in terms of the preferred role in an unambiguous way. (Giorgi, 1985, p. 60)

The steps involved in empirical phenomenological studies as outlined by von Eckartsberg (1986) follow:

Step 1: The Problem and Question Formulation—The Phenomenon. The researcher delineates a focus of investigation . . . formulates a question in such a way that it is understandable to others.
Step 2: The Data Generating Situation—The Protocol Life Text . . . researchers start with descriptive narrative provided by subjects who are viewed as co-researchers. . . . We query the person and engage in dialogue, or we combine the two.
Step 3: The Data Analysis—Explication and Interpretation. Once collected, the data are read and scrutinized so as to reveal their structure, meaning configuration, coherence, and the circumstances of their occurrence and

clustering . . . emphasis is on the study of configuration of meaning . . . involving both the structure of meaning and how it is created. (von Eckartsberg, 1986, p. 27)

I close this section on empirical phenomenological psychology with von Eckartsberg's (1986) detailing of the essential meaning structure of the experience of reconciliation.

An ongoing interpersonal relationship of intimacy and mutual importance is ruptured due to a falling out between the partners over an issue and made problematic. Ongoing face-to-face contact is disbanded and a self-righteous construal of the reasons for the break is formulated, which typically projects the blame for the break on the other partner. There is much denial. A precipitating event or crisis typically occurs in one of the partners which disrupts the stalemate and reminds that partner of the continuing claim of the relationship, of the living in tension, and in mutual rejection. Bringing the relationship to renewed awareness forces also a reconsideration of one's attitudes, values, and involvements. If one of the partners has a change of heart and/or insight into the situation and can dislodge his or her frozen and stereotyped perceptions and evaluations, owning up to and assuming some of the responsibility for the rupture, then movement toward renewed contact and conciliatory actions become possible, i.e., imaginable and actualizable.

Once initiated, the peace-making overtures must be acknowledged and reciprocated by the other so that a crucial face-to-face exchange can occur. Such an exchange involves confession of sins and stupidity, expression of regret and sorrow, and the asking of forgiveness in so many words and gestures, in a situation and moment of great vulnerability, openness, and risk. The other, when approached, has the right and choice to refuse. The accepting response of the other seals the reconciliation in a dramatic moment of mutual recognition and ongoing shared intimacy and co-creativity can resume its course in a strengthened relationship. (p. 115)

HEURISTIC RESEARCH

In my book, *Heuristic Research: Design, Methodology, and Applications* (1990), I outlined the origins of heuristic inquiry as follows:

Heuristic research came into my life when I was searching for a word that would meaningfully encompass the processes that I believed to be essential in investigations of human experience. The root meaning of *heuristic* comes from the Greek word *heuriskein*, meaning to discover or to find. It refers to a process of internal search through which one discovers the nature and meaning of experience and develops methods and procedures for further investigation and analysis. The self of the researcher is present throughout the process and, while understanding the phenomenon with increasing depth, the researcher also experiences growing self-awareness and self-knowledge. Heuristic processes incorporate creative self-processes and self-discoveries.

The cousin word of heuristic is *eureka*, exemplified by the Greek mathematician Archimedes' discovery of a principle of buoyancy. While taking a bath, he experienced a sudden, striking realization—the "aha" phenomenon—and ran naked through the streets shouting "eureka!" The process of discovery leads investigators to new images and meanings regarding human phenomena, but also to realizations relevant to their own experiences and lives. (p. 9)

As an organized and systematic form for investigating human experience, heuristic research was launched with the publication of *Loneliness* (1961) and continued in my explorations of *Loneliness and Love* (1972) and *The Touch of Loneliness* (1975). Other works influencing the development of heuristic methodology included Maslow's (1956, 1966, 1971) research on self-actualizing persons and Jourard's (1968, 1971) investigations of self-disclosure. Also of significance in the evolution of heuristic concepts are Polanyi's elucidations of the tacit dimension (Polanyi, 1964, 1966, 1969); indwelling and personal knowledge (Polanyi, 1962); Buber's (1958, 1961, 1965) explorations of dialogue and mutuality; Bridgman's (1950) delineations of subjective-objective truth; and Gendlin's (1962) analysis of meaning of experiencing. Rogers' work on human science (Coulson & Rogers, 1968; Rogers, 1969, 1985) added theoretical and conceptual depth to the heuristic paradigm presented in *Individuality and Encounter* (Moustakas, 1968) and *Rhythms, Rituals and Relationships* (Moustakas, 1981). (Moustakas, 1990, pp. 9-10)

In *Heuristic Research* (1990), I discussed the phases of heuristic research:

Heuristic inquiry is a process that begins with a question or problem which the researcher seeks to illuminate or answer. The question is one that has been a personal challenge and puzzlement in the search to understand one's self and the world in which one lives. The heuristic process is autobiographic, yet with virtually every question that matters there is also a social—and perhaps universal—significance.

Heuristics is a way of engaging in scientific search through methods and processes aimed at discovery; a way of self-inquiry and dialogue with others aimed at finding the underlying meanings of important human experiences. The deepest currents of meaning and knowledge take place within the individual through one's senses, perceptions, beliefs, and judgments. This requires a passionate, disciplined commitment to remain with a question intensely and continuously until it is illuminated or answered. (p. 15)

Six phases of heuristic research guide unfolding investigations and comprise the basic research design. They include: the initial engagement, immersion into the topic and question, incubation, illumination, explication, and culmination of the research in a creative synthesis. (p. 27)

The heuristic researcher returns again and again to the data to check the depictions of the experience to determine whether the qualities or constituents that have been derived from the data embrace the necessary and sufficient meanings. The heuristic researcher's "constant appraisal of significance" and "checking and judging" facilitate the process of achieving a valid depiction of the experience being investigated. They enable the researcher to achieve repeated verification that the explication of the phenomenon and the creative synthesis of essences and meanings actually portray the phenomenon investigated. (p. 33)

In heuristic investigations, verification is enhanced by returning to the research participants, sharing with them the meanings and essences of the phenomenon as derived from reflection on and analysis of the verbatim transcribed interviews and other material, and seeking their assessment for comprehensiveness and accuracy. (pp. 33-34)

In distinguishing the empirical phenomenological research of the Duquesne studies with that of heuristic research the following stand out:

1. Whereas the Duquesne studies focus on a situation in which the experience investigated occurs, heuristic research is a wide open investigation in which typically the research participant widely and deeply explores the phenomenon. Rarely is only one example or situation used to depict the research participants' experience.

2. Whereas in the Duquesne studies the researcher seeks descriptions of experience, in heuristics the researcher, in addition to narrative descriptions, seeks to obtain self-dialogues, stories, poems, artwork, journals and diaries, and other personal documents that *depict* the experience.

3. Whereas the Duquesne studies seek to construct structures of the experience, heuristic research aims toward composite depictions that remain

close to the individual stories rather than elucidating situational structural dynamics. Heuristic investigations culminate in a creative synthesis. Duquesne's phenomenological studies end with a general structural description.

4. Whereas in the Duquesne studies, the individual co-researchers disappear in the process of interpretation and structural analysis, in heuristics the research participants remain visible in the examination of the data and especially in the individual portraits they continue to be portrayed as whole persons. (Douglass & Moustakas, 1985)

Heuristic inquiry also differs from hermeneutic thinking. In heuristics, the focus is exclusively and continually aimed at understanding human experience. The research participants remain close to depictions of their experience, telling their individual stories with increasing understanding and insight. The depictions themselves achieve layers of depth and meaning through the interactions, explorations, and elucidations that occur between the primary researcher and the other research participants. Only the co-researchers' experiences with the phenomenon are considered, not how history, art, politics, or other human enterprises account for and explain the meanings of the experience. The life experience of the heuristic researcher and the research participants is not a text to be read or interpreted, but a comprehensive story that is portrayed in vivid, alive, accurate, and meaningful language and that is further elucidated through poems, songs, artwork, and other personal documents and creations. The depiction is complete in itself. Interpretation not only adds nothing to heuristic knowledge but removes the aliveness and vitality from the nature, roots, meanings, and essences of experience.

In organizing and synthesizing research data from heuristic studies, transcriptions of interviews, notes, poems, artwork, and personal documents are gathered together and organized by the investigator into a sequence that tells the story of each research participant. From these individual depictions, individual portraits are created that include the biographical background of the co-researcher. From the individual depictions and portraits, a composite depiction of the experience, representing the entire group of co-researchers, is developed. On the basis of his or her study of all of the depictions and portraits and personal knowledge of the experience, the primary researcher develops a creative synthesis.

Becker (1993), following the heuristic research model, studied the experience of psychiatric nurses in coping with stress at the workplace.

She conducted intensive interviews with 10 registered nurses working in the psychiatric unit of a metropolitan hospital. From her individual depictions of the nurses' experience of coping with stress, she developed the following composite depiction.

The composite depiction of an experience is developed through a process of immersion into, study of, and concentration on the experience of the phenomenon as presented by each co-researcher. At some point in this process, the qualities, core themes, and essences that permeate the experience of the entire group of co-researchers are understood and a universal depiction is constructed. (Moustakas, 1990, p. 68)

The world of the psychiatric nurse is often experienced as a place with many obstacles. The external world is experienced in a variety of ways, and one has to get through all these obstacles.

The experience of psychiatric nurses in the workplace involved meeting the expectations of others. The psychiatric nurse is holding back or unable to do or say what she really wants. The internal world of psychiatric nurses is overwhelmed with apprehension and disempowerment. Patients and other mental health workers are constantly demanding their attention. Everyone wants to extract a piece of the nurse so that she feels increasingly diminished and disabled throughout the day.

The outside world doesn't accept the psychiatric nurse, i.e., families don't feel the nurses are doing enough to improve the negative behavior of their loved ones. Families and patients are constantly asking the nurse to do the impossible. The psychiatric nurse feels frustrated and overwhelmed when she is unable to meet the patient's, family's, and hospital's demands.

This frustration and disempowerment leads to burnout. The psychiatric nurse feels unable to cope any longer with the unit stress and typically asks for a transfer to another unit. She is pressured from continuing demands by peers and mental health workers.

The internal world is very much affected and often at odds with the outside world. The nurses express their feelings that they are not given sufficient authority to use their own knowledge and experience. They describe feeling inauthentic and unable to express their real feelings, especially those of apprehension and fear.

The nurses stated that they avoid contact with the self and rarely appear as a person in interactions with patients. They must put on an act to the outside world and present themselves as brave and strong. The masking of genuine feelings, in itself creates stress, and splits the boundaries of internal and external experience. This divisiveness evokes self-doubt, and intensifies the stress. Psychiatric nurses hold back what they really think and feel, and suffer from the alienation, tension, and conflict that this creates.

On the positive side, the psychiatric nurse's ability to do what is demanded of her in the face of increasing stress and apprehension promotes a sense of being strong and enduring. In fact, this is verified by the lengthy years of service of my co-researchers and their conviction that in spite of feeling disempowered, in spite of fears and apprehensions and in spite of being overwhelmed, they are convinced they have contributed to the security, safety, and quality of life of their patients. (Becker, 1993)

COMMON QUALITIES OF HUMAN SCIENCE RESEARCH

The research models of Ethnography, Grounded Research Theory, Hermeneutics, Empirical Phenomenology, and Heuristics have been presented in this chapter. The models hold certain common features that distinguish them from traditional, natural science, quantitative research theories and methodologies. These common bonds include:

1. recognizing the value of qualitative designs and methodologies, studies of human experiences that are not approachable through quantitative approaches

2. focusing on the wholeness of experience rather than solely on its objects or parts

3. searching for meanings and essences of experience rather than measurements and explanations

4. obtaining descriptions of experience through first-person accounts in informal and formal conversations and interviews

5. regarding the data of experience as imperative in understanding human behavior and as evidence for scientific investigations

6. formulating questions and problems that reflect the interest, involvement, and personal commitment of the researcher

7. viewing experience and behavior as an integrated and inseparable relationship of subject and object and of parts and whole

Development of a transcendental phenomenological model that is the focus of this volume on phenomenological research methods also is guided by the "common bonds" listed above. Major differences exist, however, in the *launching* of a qualitative study from a transcendental phenomenological perspective and in the methods of obtaining data and methods of data analysis.

The researcher following a transcendental phenomenological approach engages in disciplined and systematic efforts to set aside prejudgments regarding the phenomenon being investigated (known as the Epoche process) in order to launch the study as far as possible free of preconceptions, beliefs, and knowledge of the phenomenon from prior experience and professional studies—to be completely open, receptive, and naive in listening to and hearing research participants describe their experience of the phenomenon being investigated.

Another major distinction is the emphasis on intuition, imagination, and universal structures in obtaining a picture of the dynamics that underlay the experience, account for, and provide an understanding of how it is that particular perceptions, feelings, thoughts, and sensual awarenesses are evoked in consciousness with reference to a specific experience such as jealousy, anger, or joy. The methods of analysis of the transcendental phenomenological model presented in this volume also distinguish it from other research approaches.

The chapters that follow present in detail the transcendental phenomenological model—theory, concepts, processes, design, methodology, and examples of my own development and applications of the model as the guiding framework for conducting human science research.

REFERENCES

Addison, R. B. (1989). Grounded interpreted research: An investigation of physician socialization. In M. J. Parker & R. B. Addison (Eds.), *Entering the circle: Hermeneutic investigation in psychology* (pp. 39-57). New York: SUNY Press.

Becker, J. (1993). *The experience of psychiatric nurses coping with stress at the workplace.* Unpublished doctoral dissertation, The Union Institute, Cincinnati, OH.

Benedict, R. (1959). *Patterns of culture.* New York: New American Library.

Bogdan, R., & Taylor, S. (1975). *Introduction to qualitative research methods.* New York: John Wiley.

Bridgman, P. (1950). *Reflections of a physicist.* New York: Philosophical Library.

Buber, M. (1958). *I and thou.* New York: Scribners.

Buber, M. (1961). *Tales of Hasidim: The early masters* (O. Marx, Trans.). New York: Schocken.

Buber, M. (1965). *The knowledge of man.* New York: Harper & Row.

Coulson, W., & Rogers, C. R. (Eds.). (1968). *Man and the science of man.* Columbus, OH: Charles E. Merrill.

DiGregorio, J. (1983). *A psychological investigation of deinstitutionalization.* Doctoral dissertation, Union for Experimenting Colleges and Universities, 1983. (University Microfilms International, 8404643).

Dilthey, W. (1976). *Selected writings* (H. P. Rickman, Ed. & Trans.). Cambridge: Cambridge University Press.

Douglass, B., & Moustakas, C. (1985). Heuristic inquiry: The internal search to know. *Journal of Humanistic Psychology, 25*(3), 39-55.

Gadamer, H. G. (1976). *Philosophical hermeneutics* (D. E. Linge, Ed. & Trans.). Berkeley: University of California Press.

Gadamer, H. G. (1984). The hermeneutics of suspicion. In G. Shapiro & A. Sica (Eds.), *Hermeneutics: Questions and prospects* (pp. 54-65). Amherst: University of Massachusetts Press.

Gendlin, E. (1962). *Experiencing and the creation of meaning.* Chicago: Free Press.

Giorgi, A. (1979). The relationships among level, type, and structure and their importance for social science theorizing: A dialogue with Shutz. In A. Giorgi, R. Knowles, & D. L. Smith (Eds.), *Duquesne studies in phenomenological psychology* (Vol. 3, pp. 81-92). Pittsburgh: Duquesne University Press.

Giorgi, A. (Ed.). (1985). *Phenomenology and psychological research.* Pittsburgh: Duquesne University Press.

Giorgi, A., Fischer, W. F., & Von Eckartsberg, R. (Eds.). (1971). *Duquesne studies in phenomenological psychology* (Vol. 1). Pittsburgh: Duquesne University Press.

Giorgi, A., Fischer, C., & Murray, E. (1975). *Duquesne studies in phenomenological psychology* (Vol. 2). Pittsburgh: Duquesne University Press.

Giorgi, A., Knowles, R., & Smith, D. L. (Eds.). (1979). *Duquesne studies in phenomenological psychology* (Vol. 3). Pittsburgh: Duquesne University Press.

Giorgi, A., Barton, A., & Maes, C. (Eds.). (1983). *Duquesne studies in phenomenological psychology* (Vol. 4). Pittsburgh: Duquesne University Press.

Glaser, B., & Strauss, A. L. (1967). *The discovery of grounded theory: Strategies for qualitative research.* New York: Adeline.

Holmes, P. (1993). *The experience of homelessness.* Unpublished doctoral dissertation, The Union Institute, Cincinnati, OH.

Jager, B. (1979). Dionysius and the world of passion. In A. Giorgi, R. Knowles, & D. L. Smith (Eds.), *Duquesne studies in phenomenological psychology* (Vol. 3, pp. 209-226). Pittsburgh: Duquesne University Press.

Jorgensen, D. L. (1989). *Participant-observation: A method for human studies.* Newbury Park, CA: Sage.

Jourard, S. (1968). *Disclosing man to himself.* New York: Van Nostrand.

Jourard, S. (1971). *Self-disclosure: An experimental analysis of the transparent self.* New York: Wiley-Interscience.

Lofland, J. (1971). *Analyzing social settings.* Belmont, CA: Wadsworth.

Makkreel, R. A. (1975). *Dilthey: Philosophies of the human studies.* Princeton, NJ: Princeton University Press.

Maslow, A. H. (1956). Self-actualizing people: A study of psychological health. In C. Moustakas (Ed.), *The self* (pp. 160-194). New York: Harper & Brothers.

Maslow, A. H. (1966). *The psychology of science.* New York: Harper & Row.

Maslow, A. H. (1971). *The farther reaches of human nature.* New York: Viking.

Mead, M. (1928). *Coming of age in Samoa.* New York: William C. Morrow.

Mead, M. (1975). *Growing up in New Guinea.* New York: William C. Morrow.

Montgomery, C. L. (1990). Nurse's perceptions of significant caring communication encounters. *Dissertation Abstracts International, 51-07A*, 2198. (University Microfilms No. AAD 90-300091)

Montgomery, C. L. (1991). The care-giving relationship: Paradoxical and transcendent aspects. *The Journal of Transpersonal Psychology, 13*(2), 91-104.

Moustakas, C. (1961). *Loneliness.* Englewood Cliffs, NJ: Prentice Hall.

Moustakas, C. (1968). *Individuality and encounter.* Cambridge, MA: Howard Doyle.

Moustakas, C. (1972). *Loneliness and love.* Englewood Cliffs, NJ: Prentice Hall.

Moustakas, C. (1975). *The touch of loneliness.* Englewood Cliffs, NJ: Prentice Hall.

Moustakas, C. (1981). *Rhythms, rituals, and relationships.* Detroit, MI: Center for Humanistic Studies.

Moustakas, C. (1990). *Heuristic research: Design, methodology, and applications.* Newbury Park, CA: Sage.

Patton, M. (1990). *Qualitative evaluation and research methods.* Newbury Park, CA: Sage.

Polanyi, M. (1962). *Personal knowledge.* Chicago: University of Chicago Press.

Polanyi, M. (1964). *Science, faith and society.* Chicago: University of Chicago Press.

Polanyi, M. (1966). *The tacit dimension.* Garden City, NY: Doubleday.

Polanyi, M. (1969). *Knowing and being* (M. Grene, Ed.). Chicago: University of Chicago Press.

Rogers, C. R. (1969). Toward a science of the person. In A. J. Sutich & M. A. Vich (Eds.), *Readings in humanistic psychology* (pp. 21-50). New York: Macmillan.

Rogers, C. R. (1985). Toward a more human science of the person. *Journal of Humanistic Psychology, 24*(4), 7-24.

Strauss, A., & Corbin, J. (1990). *Basics of qualitative research: Grounded theory, procedures and techniques.* Newbury Park, CA: Sage.

Strauss, A. L. (1987). *Qualitative analysis for social scientists.* New York: Cambridge University Press.

Titelman, P. (1979). Some implications of Ricoeur's conception of hermeneutics for phenomenological psychology. In A. Giorgi, R. Knowles, & D. L. Smith (Eds.), *Duquesne studies in phenomenological psychology* (Vol. 3, pp. 182-192). Pittsburgh: Duquesne University Press.

van Kaam, A. (1959). Phenomenal analysis: Exemplified by a study of the experience of "really feeling understood." *Journal of Individual Psychology, 15*(1), 66-72.

van Kaam, A. (1966). *Existential foundations of psychology.* Pittsburgh: Duquesne University Press.

Van Maanen, J. (1982). Fieldwork on the beat. In J. Van Maanen, J. M. Dabbs, & R. R. Faulkner (Eds.), *Varieties of qualitative research* (pp. 103-151). Beverly Hills, CA: Sage.

Van Maanen, J., Dabbs, J. M., Jr., & Faulkner, R. R. (1982). *Varieties of qualitative research.* Beverly Hills, CA: Sage.

von Eckartsberg, R. (1986). *Life-world experience: Existential-phenomenological research approaches to psychology.* Washington, DC: Center for Advanced Research in Phenomenology & University Press of America.

Wolf, D. R. (1991). High-risk methodology: Reflections on leaving an outlaw society. In W. B. Shaffir & R. A. Stebbins (Eds.), *Experiencing fieldwork* (pp. 211-223). Newbury Park, CA: Sage.

TRANSCENDENTAL PHENOMENOLOGY
Conceptual Framework

In this reflective meditation on transcendental phenomenology, I especially recognize Edmund Husserl, who stood alone, a determined self-presence, pioneering new realms of philosophy and science. He developed a philosophic system rooted in subjective openness, a radical approach to science that was criticized and laughed at; yet throughout his professional life Husserl remained strong, continuing to expand his ideas, and finally responding with silence to all those critics who held onto their own fixed philosophies and saw only the weaknesses and inadequacies of Husserl's thinking. Husserl himself realized that his work would be of no value to closed minds, to those who have not known the despair of "one who has the misfortune to be in love with philosophy" (1931, p. 29). This being "in love with philosophy" captures me also and evokes a desire to employ phenomenology in discoveries of knowledge and in theories and applications of human science.

For a while, I became an isolate, in the way that Husserl advised, withdrawing completely into myself, while seeking to acquire knowledge of science through concentrated studies of experience and the reflective powers of the self. I sought to place myself in Husserl's world of transcendental phenomenology, while recognizing that my own knowledge and experience, in a free, open, and imaginative sense, ultimately would determine the core ideas and values that would linger and endure. According to Kockelmans (1967, p. 24), the term *phenomenology* was used as early as 1765 in philosophy and occasionally in Kant's writings, but only with Hegel was a well-defined technical meaning constructed. For Hegel, phenomenology referred to knowledge as it appears to consciousness, the science of describing what one perceives, senses, and knows in one's immediate awareness and experience. The process leads to an unfolding of phenomenal consciousness through science and philosophy "toward the absolute knowledge of the Absolute" (Kockelmans, 1967, p. 24).

It was not Hegel, however, but Descartes who influenced Husserl in a dominant sense, and specifically Husserl's development of the concept of Epoche. Epoche requires the elimination of suppositions and the raising of knowledge above every possible doubt. For Husserl, as for Kant and Descartes, knowledge based on intuition and essence precedes empirical knowledge. Although the doubt of Descartes was transformed into the Epoche of Husserl, both philosophers recognized the crucial value of returning to the self to discover the nature and meaning of things as they appear and in their essence. Only one source of certainty exists, what I think, what I feel, in substance, what I perceive (Lauer, 1967, p. 155). Husserl asserted that, "Ultimately, all genuine, and, in particular, all scientific knowledge, rests on inner evidence: as far as such evidence extends, the concept of knowledge extends also" (1970, p. 61).

What appears in consciousness is the phenomenon. The word *phenomenon* comes from the Greek *phaenesthai,* to flare up, to show itself, to appear. Constructed from *phaino,* phenomenon means to bring to light, to place in brightness, to show itself in itself, the totality of what lies before us in the light of day (Heidegger, 1977, pp. 74-75). Thus, the maxim of phenomenology, "To the things themselves." In a broad sense that which appears provides the impetus for experience and for generating new knowledge. Phenomena are the building blocks of human science and the basis for all knowledge.

Any phenomenon represents a suitable starting point for an investigation. What is given in our perception of a thing is its appearance, yet this is not an empty illusion. It serves as the essential beginning of a science that seeks valid determinations that are open to anyone to verify (Husserl, 1931, p. 129).

The intertwining of subjective and objective knowledge in Husserl's thinking was also influenced by Descartes's (1912/1988) posture on objective reality, that "the object is said to possess objective reality insofar as it exists by representation in thought . . . ; for objective reality (i.e., the reality of representation) is in truth a subjective reality" (1912/1988, p. 249). In other words, perception of the reality of an object is dependent on a subject.

Husserl was concerned with the discovery of meanings and essences in knowledge. He believed that a sharp contrast exists between facts and essences, between the real and non-real. He asserted that, "Essence provides on the one side a knowledge of the essential nature of the Real, on the other, in respect of the domain left over, knowledge of the essential nature of the non-real (*irreal*)" (1931, p. 45).

The challenge facing the human science researcher is to describe things in themselves, to permit what is before one to enter consciousness and be understood in its meanings and essences in the light of intuition and self-reflection. The process involves a blending of what is really present with what is imagined as present from the vantage point of possible meanings; thus a unity of the real and the ideal.

The transformation of individual or empirical experience into essential insights occurs through a special process that Husserl calls "ideation" (Kockelmans, 1967, p. 80). The object that appears in consciousness mingles with the object in nature so that a meaning is created, and knowledge is extended. Thus a relationship exists between what exists in conscious awareness and what exists in the world. What appears in consciousness is an absolute reality while what appears in the world is a product of learning.

Husserl (1931) offers this example of the intentional object appearing in consciousness and the object given in nature.

> In front of me, in the dim light, lies this white paper. I see it, touch it. This perceptual seeing and touching of the paper as the full concrete experience *of* the paper that lies here as given in truth precisely . . . with this relative lack of clearness, with this imperfect definition, appearing to me from this particular angle—is a *cogitatio*, a conscious experience. The paper itself with its objective qualities, its extension in space, its objective position in regard to that spatial thing I call my body, is not *cogitatio*, but *cogitatum*, not perceptual experience, but something perceived. (p. 116) [This and other quotes from this work are reprinted by permission of Unwin Hyman.]

Husserl (1977) does not claim that transcendental phenomenology is the only approach to a knowledge of human experience, but rather he emphasizes that it is a science of pure possibilities carried out with systematic concreteness and that it precedes, and makes possible, the empirical sciences, the sciences of actualities (p. 72).

INTENTIONALITY

Husserl's transcendental phenomenology is intimately bound up in the concept of intentionality. In Aristotelian philosophy the term *intention* indicates the orientation of the mind to its object; the object exists in the mind in an intentional way (Kockelmans, 1967, p. 32). With reference to perceiving, the intentional act "is the perceiving of something . . . judging, the judging of a certain matter; valuation, the valuing of a value; wish, the wish for the content wished" (Husserl, 1931, p. 243).

Husserl advanced Brentano's assertion that "intentionality is the fundamental characteristic of 'psychic phenomena' "—the groundwork for a descriptive transcendental philosophy of consciousness (Husserl, 1977, p. 41). Although Brentano believed that when an individual perceptually experiences an object the object always exists, Husserl held to the position that the object may be imaginary and not exist at all. Both men were in agreement that *directedness* is an intrinsic feature of intentionality, that the mind is directed toward some entity whether the entity exists or not. The object, whether real or imaginary, is anything toward which a need may be directed (Miller, 1984, p. 223).

Intentionality refers to consciousness, to the internal experience of being conscious of something; thus the act of consciousness and the object of consciousness are intentionally related. Included in an understanding of consciousness are important background factors; such as, stirrings of pleasure, early shapings of judgment, or incipient wishes (Husserl, 1931, pp. 243-244).

Knowledge of intentionality requires that we be present to ourselves and to things in the world, that we recognize that self and world are inseparable components of meaning. As Kockelmans (1967) points out, "Consciousness itself cannot be anything other than openness, directedness to the other. . . . In this way consciousness appears to be not pure interiority, but should be understood as a going-out-of-itself" (p. 36).

Intentional acts are objectifying while feeling acts are non-objectifying. Smith (1981, p. 87) introduces the intentional act of perceiving the night sky with the feeling act of wonder. The perception of a night sky may remain even when the feeling of wonder disappears. The night sky remains open as a concrete, independent, intentional experience, while the feeling-act of wonder may or may not continue to exist.

The following example, also from Smith (1981, p. 88), illustrates the acts of consciousness. Consider the experience of joy on witnessing a beautiful landscape. The landscape is the *matter*. The landscape is also the object of the intentional act, for example, of perception in consciousness. The matter enables the landscape to become manifest as an object rather than merely exist in consciousness.

The *interpretive form* is the perception that enables the landscape to appear; thus the landscape is self-given; my perception creates it and enables it to exist in my consciousness. The *objectifying quality* is the actuality of the landscape's existence, as such, while the *non-objectifying quality* is the joyful feeling evoked in me by the landscape.

Every intentionality is comprised of a *noema* and *noesis*. The noema is not the real object but the phenomenon, not the tree but the appearance of the tree. The object that appears in perception varies in terms of when it is perceived, from what angle, with what background of experience, with what orientation of wishing, willing, or judging, always from the vantage point of a perceiving individual (Gurwitsch, 1967, p. 128). Gurwitsch points out that different perceptions "enter into a synthesis of identification with one another . . . into this real thing which it is" (p. 129). From whatever angle as one views an object, from front, side, or back, the synthesis of perceptions, for example, means that a tree will continue to present itself as the same real tree. The tree is out there present in time and space while the perception of the tree is in consciousness. Regardless of when or how, regardless of which components or what perception, memory, wish, or judgment, the synthesis of noemata (perceived meanings) enable the experiencing person to continue to see the tree as just this tree and no other.

Every intentional experience is also noetic; "it is its essential nature to harbour in itself a 'meaning' of some sort, it may be many meanings" (Husserl, 1931, p. 257). Through the original noesis, the initial underlying meaning, further phases may be developed, which themselves become meaningful (Husserl, 1931, p. 257).

In considering the noema-noesis correlate, the question remains:

What is the "perceived as such"? What essential phases does it harbor in itself in its capacity as noema? We win the reply to our question as we wait, in pure surrender, on what is essentially *given*. We can then describe "that which appears as such" faithfully and in the light of perfect self-evidence. (Husserl, 1931, p. 260)

The "perceived as such" is the noema; the "perfect self-evidence" is the noesis. Their relationship constitutes the intentionality of consciousness. For every noema there is a noesis; for every noesis there is a noema. On the noematic side is the uncovering and explication, the unfolding and becoming distinct, the clearing of what is actually presented in consciousness. On the noetic side is an explication of the intentional processes themselves (Husserl, 1977, p. 46). What is meant noematically is continually changing in perception, the something meant is more, more than what is originally meant explicitly. The something meant achieves a synthesis through a continual perceiving of the whole throughout its angular visions and perceptions.

For example, the immediate, spontaneous noematic meanings that I associate with a physician's recommendation of drugs as a way of resolving bodily tensions are suspicion, doubt, images of physical and mental consequences, invasion of my body by harmful chemicals, interference with my natural healing processes, control of my destiny by external forces, direction of my life from an authority who lacks adequate evidence that what he or she is recommending will help rather than harm, awareness that placebos are often as effective as drugs, and arousal of residual consequences that interfere with eating, sleeping, and other important experiences.

When I consider the noetic factors that account for my noematic meanings, I recall my experience with two physicians who injected drugs into my body when I was experiencing considerable pain from infections. In one instance, my face ballooned so that I was unable to open my mouth and was disabled for about 3 days—until the drug was out of my system and natural healing processes were activated. In the second experience, further accentuating noematic meanings connected with drugs, I experienced pronounced disorientation when I used drugs prescribed by a physician to control neck and back pain caused by an auto accident. I was unable to focus without considerable effort. I distorted distances. I was unable to drive. Another noetic emphasis occurred as I witnessed my sister's extreme deterioration over a period of several months when drugs were repeatedly used to control her hallucinations. The drugs ultimately destroyed her rational and occupational skills and her ability to control bodily functions. I believe they killed her at an early age.

The working out of the noema-noesis relationship, the textural (noe- ᵠ matic) and structural (noetic) dimensions of phenomena, and the derivation of meanings is an essential function of intentionality. Brand (1967) observes that, "In each experience, intentionality functions simultaneously as implicit pro-ject (*Vor-wurf*) and as retro-spect (*Ruck-schau*)" (p. 198). In the beginning, functioning intentionality is completely anonymous; it is concealed; "its quiddities are still wrapped up, not yet unfolded" (Brand, 1967, p. 199). In the grasping of the meaning of experience,we are engaging in a process of functioning intentionality; we uncover the meanings of phenomena, deliver them from the anonymity of the natural attitude, move them toward an inclusive totality of consciousness. Gurwitsch (1967) offers the following example in clarifying the noema-noesis relationship, the correlates of intentionality.

Let us assume now that I perceive this particular house from the street in front of it so that I can effectively see only its facade. If, subsequently, I want to learn more about this house's exterior appearance, then the only possibility is to have recourse to ever-new "partial perceptions," each of which will manifest separately a certain aspect of this house . . . the perceived thing clearly does not exhaust itself in any one of its individual profiles, but that which is intended in each of the concrete acts, without, however, being effectively and as such perceived in any particular act whatsoever remains the same in all cases. In this particular act of perception or *noesis* this house effectively manifests itself always in this particular profile when this particular standpoint is assumed; but, nonetheless, each concrete act intends more than this particular profile and aims at the house as a whole. (Gurwitsch, 1967, pp. 140-141)

Summarizing the challenges of intentionality, the following processes stand out:

1. Explicating the sense in which our experiences are directed;
2. Discerning the features of consciousness that are essential for the individuation of objects (real or imaginary) that are before us in consciousness (Noema);

3. Explicating how beliefs about such objects (real or imaginary) may be acquired, how it is that we are experiencing what we are experiencing (Noesis) (Miller, 1984, p. 8); and

4. Integrating the noematic and noetic correlates of intentionality into meanings and essences of experience.

INTUITION

Intuition is another key concept of transcendental phenomenology. Descartes (1977) held intuition to be primary, an inborn talent directed "toward producing solid and true judgments concerning everything that presents itself" (p. 22). This "presents itself" was the starting point for Descartes, as it was for Husserl in his return to things themselves. Further, for Descartes, intuition was regarded as a distinct capacity of a pure and attentive mind born from "the light of reason alone" (pp. 28-29). Thus intuition is the beginning place in deriving knowledge of human experience, free of everyday sense impressions and the natural attitude.

Whatever else may enter into my awareness, my intuitive knowing of myself and what presents itself of its own accord does not betray me. No one can convince me, "that I am nothing as long as I shall think myself to be something . . . *I am, I exist,* every time it is pronounced by me, or mentally conceived, necessarily is true" (Descartes, 1977, p. 197).

The self for Descartes and for Husserl is an intuitive-thinking being, a being who doubts, understands, affirms, denies, wishes for or against, senses, imagines. All things become clear and evident through an intuitive-reflective process, through a transformation of what is seen; first intuitively in the common appearance, in the manner in which something is presented and then in the fullness and clarity of an intuitive-reflective process. By stripping away something of its garments, by abstaining from the natural attitude, the everyday knowing of things, by considering something in its naked presence, "as it truly is—when I do this, although there can still be an error in my judgment, nevertheless I cannot perceive it," in its essence except with my own mind, which is me, myself (Descartes, 1977, p. 202). As I come to know this thing before me, I also come to know myself as the being who intuits, reflects, judges, and understands.

Unlike Descartes, Husserl did not employ deduction in his transcendental philosophy; only intuition was utilized. Intuition is essential in describing whatever presents itself, whatever is actually given. For Husserl intuition "is the presence to consciousness of an essence, with all that that implies by way of necessity and universal validity" (Lauer, 1967, p. 153). Husserl identified a priori knowledge with the intuition of pure essences. He recognized the imperative of intuition in the self-givenness of objects (Levinas, 1967, pp. 90-91).

METHODOLOGY OF TRANSCENDENTAL PHENOMENOLOGY

The methodology of Transcendental Phenomenology will be considered in much more detail in a future chapter. In this section I will briefly discuss the core processes that facilitate derivation of knowledge: Epoche, Transcendental-Phenomenological Reduction, and Imaginative Variation.

Epoche is a Greek word meaning to refrain from judgment, to abstain from or stay away from the everyday, ordinary way of perceiving things. In the natural attitude we hold knowledge judgmentally; we presuppose that what we perceive in nature is actually there and remains there as we perceive it. In contrast, Epoche requires a new way of looking at things, a way that requires that we learn *to see* what stands before our eyes, what we can distinguish and describe.

In essence, every experience

> however far it extends, leaves open the possibility that what is given, despite the persistent consciousness of its bodily self-presence, does *not* exist . . . *existence in the form of a thing is never demanded as necessary by virtue of its givenness* . . . the further course of experience will compel us to abandon what has already been set down and justified *in the light of empirical canons of rightness. . . . The thesis of my pure Ego and its personal life, which is "necessary" and plainly indubitable, thus stands opposed to the thesis of the world.* (Husserl, 1931, pp. 144-145)

In the Epoche, the everyday understandings, judgments, and knowings are set aside, and phenomena are revisited, freshly, naively, in a wide open sense, from the vantage point of a pure or transcendental ego.

The Epoche is a necessary first step. Following the Epoche, the next essential process is the Transcendental-Phenomenological Reduction. It is called transcendental because it moves beyond the everyday to the pure ego in which everything is perceived freshly, as if for the first time. "It is called 'phenomenological' because it transforms the world into mere phenomena. It is called 'reduction' because it leads us back (Lat. *reducere*) to the source of the meaning and existence of the experienced world" (Schmitt, 1967, p. 61).

In the Transcendental-Phenomenological Reduction, each experience is considered in its singularity, in and for itself. The phenomenon is perceived and described in its totality, in a fresh and open way. A complete description is given of its essential constituents, variations of perceptions, thoughts, feelings, sounds, colors, and shapes.

Ultimately, through the Transcendental-Phenomenological Reduction we derive a textural description of the meanings and essences of the phenomenon, the constituents that comprise the experience in consciousness, from the vantage point of an open self. From this perspective, "the content of experience is dependent on myself as subject; experience presents to me its claim to validity: I must certify this claim . . . I, as a subject, (am) . . . not only the source of validity of experience, but also of its significance" (Schmitt, 1967, p. 67).

A moving example of the phenomenological reduction is included in Wertz's (1985) study of the experience of being criminally victimized. Removing repetitive statements, Wertz presents one co-researcher's description of the experience.

> I was coming home late at night and had a car behind me. I didn't think much of it because there are a lot of cars coming down that road at that time. It followed me into the parking lot and parked at the end of the lot. I thought it was our neighbor's car because it looked the same. I parked right in front of our building and got out. When I got to the steps, I turned around because I didn't hear car doors and I always got a fear over my shoulder. He was right at my feet—must have really flew. He grabbed me to pick me up by my ankles and throw me over his shoulder. I was very shocked, never thought it would happen to me. He got up that far and it was wintertime and I had a fur coat on so he couldn't—and I just collapsed out of fear. My legs went—I guess I was dead weight and he dropped me. I hung onto the railing and just screamed. I kept my legs together and I didn't know what he was trying to do but he kept going up my legs or something. He was trying to pull me away from the railing. I saw his car parked with the open door, and there was another guy in the car. He attempted to put me in his

car, but he didn't succeed. He must have seen I was alone and followed me. (p. 168)

The Imaginative Variation follows the Transcendental-Phenomenological Reduction. Its aim is to grasp the structural essences of experience. Descartes (1977) presents a forerunner idea to Husserl's emphasis on free fantasy variation, essential to the Imaginative Variation. He states that "the intellect ought to use every assistance of the imagination, sense, and memory: to intuit distinctly . . . and to correctly unite what is sought after with what is known in order that the former may be distinguished" (1977, p. 57). In *Ideas,* Husserl (1931) makes a similar statement: "The Eidos, *the pure essence,* can be exemplified intuitively in the data of experience, data of perception, memory and so forth, but just as readily *also in the mere data of fancy* (Phantasie)" (p. 57).

The function of the Imaginative Variation is to arrive at a "*structural differentiation among the infinite multiplicities* of actual and possible *cognitiones,* that relate to the object in question and thus can somehow go together to make up the unity of an identifying synthesis" (Husserl, 1977, p. 63). From this process a structural description of the essences of the experience is derived, presenting a picture of the conditions that precipitate an experience and connect with it. An example of the experience of being anxious is excerpted from Fischer's (1989) study.

An anxious situation arises when the self-understanding in which one is genuinely invested is rendered problematically uncertain and hence, possibly untrue. Two variations of this situation may be delineated: In the first, an essential constituent of that self-understanding, one that expresses one's identification with a state of affairs that one is endeavoring to realize, for example, becoming a PhD candidate in one's graduate program, is now experienced as possibly unattainable, and thus the entire self-understanding that one is living is called into question; in the second, a meaning that one is living as either never-to-be true-of-one or as no-longer-to-be-true-of-one, for example, being someone who "gives in" to the desire to masturbate, has emerged as possibly (still) true, thereby undermining the self-understanding that is, at least in part, founded upon its absolute exclusion.

Initially, becoming and being anxious in either of these situations means that one experiences a sudden loss of momentum, a sense of being blocked, an inability to move forward undividedly. Confronted with multiple, problematic, and often contradictory meanings of the situation, one is captured, at least temporarily, by its ambiguity, its lack of a univocal meaning. Expressing this sense of being blocked and captured is a burgeoning uncertainty as to what to do, for that matter, as to one's ability to do anything effectively.

Breaking through this more or less articulate confusion, one experiences the alien, dysfunctional character of one's body as it resonates to the uncertainties of the situation. It is important to note that how one relates to these bodily resonances, for example, the dryness of one's mouth, the feeling of weakness in one's knees, and/or the sense of "butterflies" in one's stomach will prefigure whether one will explicitly acknowledge and feel one's anxiousness. Moreover, even if that anxiousness is explicitly acknowledged and felt, one may not take it up with an interest in genuinely discovering its significations, that is, take it up as revealing something important about the present situation and one's projects thereof.

Most typically, one will make an effort to turn away from what one's body is announcing. That is, one may engage in a flurry of action, usually aggressive, directed at some aspect of the problematic situation, for example, at an other or at some aspect of oneself in the form of disparagements. Or, one may acknowledge the fact of one's anxiousness but refuse to recognize, let alone explore, the situation at its reciprocally implied source. Hence, to state the matter somewhat differently, one may not allow one's anxious body explicitly to signify the problematic significance of the situation.

Beyond this general characterization, two diverse styles of being anxious may be delineated. In the first, one feels paralyzed, in imminent danger of being overwhelmed by the unthinkable, the inescapably problematic character of one's self-understanding; one is unable to even consider its implications. Hence, one continues, often adamantly, to turn away from the possibility of reflecting upon it. The situation is lived as if there was nothing to be learned from it; nothing has really changed, only the familiar is acknowledged. (Fischer, 1989, pp. 134-135) [Reprinted by permission of the editors]

In the phenomenological model that I employ, the structural essences of the Imaginative Variation are then integrated with the textural essences of the Transcendental-Phenomenological Reduction in order to arrive at a textural-structural synthesis of meanings and essences of the phenomenon or experience being investigated.

INTERSUBJECTIVITY

Although Husserl recognized the imperative of the transcendental ego in the uncovering of meanings and essences, he did not ignore the importance of the intersubjective, particularly in connection with self-insights and subjective perceptions of what is real. Husserl states, "I *experience* the world (including others) and, according to its experiential sense, not as (so to speak) my *private* synthetic formation but as other than mine alone (mir Frende), as an *intersubjective* world, actually there for everyone, accessible in respect of its Objects to everyone" (1977, p. 91). The method through which the Other becomes accessible to me is that of empathy, a thereness-for-me of others. Empathy is an intentional category comprising my experience of others' experience (Lauer, 1967, p. 172).

The Other is not directly within me. Otherwise, Husserl (1977) asserts, the Other and I would be the same (p. 109). Thus my relationship to the Other is that of a copresence. I am aware that there is another body coexisting with my body and of similar appearance. This makes possible the analogizing apprehension "of that body as another animate organism" (Husserl, 1977, p. 111). Through analogy, I apprehend the other in a livingly present sense. "*Ego* and *alter ego* are always and necessarily given in an original 'pairing' " (Husserl, 1977, p. 112). "Pairing" is the way in which I experience someone else. In "pairing," the Other is within me and I within the Other. My existence and the Other's existence are copresent in intentional communion. This community sense exists as possibility in every human being. In principle, there is within me a realm of virtually infinite access to other human beings.

I must first explicate my own intentional consciousness through transcendental processes before I can understand someone or something that is not my own, someone or something that is apprehended analogically. My own perception is primary; it includes the perception of the other by analogy.

Framing intersubjectivity in this way overcomes the illusion of solipsism. Husserl believed that the "solipsism is dissolved, *even though* the proposition that everything existing for me must derive its existential sense exclusively from me myself, from my sphere of consciousness" (1977, p. 150).

Another aspect of intersubjectivity is contained in Farber's (1943) contention that in experience, by analogy, others become present to me to the extent that they enter my consciousness, are copresent to me, and become essential to my intentional experience. Schutz (1967) adds an important clarification.

If I look at my whole stock of your lived experiences and ask about the structure of this knowledge, one thing becomes clear: *This is that everything I know about your conscious life is really based on my knowledge of my own lived experiences.* *My* lived experiences *of* you are constituted in simultaneity or quasisimultaneity with *your* lived experiences, to which they are intentionally related. It is only because of this that, when I look backward, I am able to synchronize *my* past experiences of you with *your* past experiences. (p. 106)

APPLICATION TO ENHANCING IDENTITY

In my seminars at the University College of Cape Breton in Nova Scotia, I have engaged my graduate students in experiences of Epoche, Phenomenological Reduction, and Imaginative Variation. Each student is invited to establish a special relationship with a child or adolescent, aiming toward recognizing, supporting, and enhancing the identity of this person.

As a way of preparing my students (who are elementary and secondary teachers), I have asked them to reflect on what constitutes an ideal relationship. When an inner receptiveness is achieved, the teachers are able to bring their concept of an ideal relationship into consciousness. They are then able to focus on the features or qualities of a person who had enhanced their identity. I have suggested the following:

1. Describe briefly the nature of the relationship.
2. Select one episode, event, or situation in which your own sense of being recognized, accepted, and valued stood out.
3. Describe the qualities of this other person who awakened in you feelings of self-esteem and self-confidence. Develop a unified descriptive portrait of this person's relationship to you.
4. Look over your descriptive portrait and determine whether you have included everything of significance. Elaborate on the description, if needed.

Each teacher joins a small group and shares his or her ideal "person-in-relationship." A list of dominant qualities is developed and reduced to nonrepetitive meanings. A composite portrait of the person who successfully enhances identity is then constructed. Each small group presents its composite portrait to the total class. Overlapping and repetitive qualities are eliminated until a "total class" composite portrait is arrived at, representing the core qualities or meanings that will enhance the identity of a child or adolescent in a relationship. This then becomes a model that guides teachers as they develop a special relationship with a child or adolescent in their own classrooms.

The composite portraits, derived from my graduate students, have been similar each year that I have taught this seminar but the synthesis of an ideal relationship has its own phrasing, style, emphasis, and organization, and holds a different kind of significance and meaning as teachers participate in processes of Epoche, Reduction, and Imaginative Variation. In a recent composite portrait, the "ideal" teacher recognizes the child or adolescent as an incomparable being, believes in him or her and enables this person to feel special, distinctive, and unique. The enhancer of identity encourages individual differences; instills confidence; supports the child's or adolescent's right to make choices and pursue self-chosen activities. The child's individuality is encouraged through opportunities and resources made available by the enhancer. He or she listens and hears accurately; perceives meanings from the child's or adolescent's frame of reference; offers suggestions but does not impose; values the thoughts, feelings, and preferences of the child or adolescent; and communicates in direct and honest language. The enhancer creates an atmosphere of freedom, openness, and trust, and is willing to respond and disclose his or her own thoughts and feelings. The enhancer enters the child's or adolescent's world; provides a space and clearing; listens to understand, recognize, and support; and offers a point of view or assessment when asked. She or he affirms interests, needs, and desires; rhythmically connects with the mood or state of mind of the child or adolescent; shares activities; and, where relevant, makes available special resources for art work, movement, storytelling, and drama.

With a composite portrait of the person who enhances identity as a guide, the following is an example of the outcome in one relationship.

Norman, one of my seminar teachers, in his first meeting with Louise, learned that she felt at home in places of nature and solitude. He also learned that she was 9 years old, was shy, and preferred silence to talk. During the summer session, he chose Louise to begin to establish the ideal relationship. He asked her if she would be interested in meeting with him for a trip to a nearby beach. She responded affirmatively. Her parents granted permission. The verbatim chronicle follows.

Louise and I walked on the sand in silence except for the sound of the sea gulls. . . . I learned that her silence is an outcome of shyness. When we had walked some while, she began to refer to her school experiences and her disappointment in what was being taught, the lack of freedom and time to learn things of value to her. I asked her if school was the only place for learning. I sensed that she was aware that life itself outside the classroom tapped her ability to learn. She immediately pointed to the beach, sand and water and what could be learned through observation. I asked what she had learned. To my surprise she literally shouted, "Do you really want to know? Sometimes big people don't want to hear what children have to say." I assured her that I was not only interested but had no other interest while with her but to listen and understand her.

She began to open up in a way that I never thought would happen. She said she loved being at the beach, noticing things, the smoothness of the rocks from the constant work of sand and water going over and over them thousands and millions of times. The rocks called to her, fascinated her, told her stories of movement from the bottom of the ocean, of shifting shapes, sizes, colors, affected by the intense, continuing sun shine and by heavy wind storms. She pointed to large pieces of driftwood which she said originally came from trees hanging over the edge of cliffs overlooking water. Wind and rain pushed the tree limbs into the ocean and after some time onto the beach, worn, weathered, lined, bleached. She then invited me to join her in skipping small flat rocks on top of the water. With fine rhythm and motion her rocks skipped far out to sea, six to eight times. She said "the sea is here to give fish and other food things, and a place to swim, sail, and play."

Our meetings passed quickly. We wrote in the sand, drew pictures, and watched intently as the waves washed our creations away.

I believe that Louise felt good, free, open, expressive in my presence. I learned to listen, to sense her meanings, to express my interest and valuing of her. I have no doubt that my meetings with her were but a beginning but in itself of value in recognizing and supporting her, her initiative and way of being. She alternated silence and talk and entrusted me with some of the things that mattered most in her life.

SUMMARY AND CONCLUSION

The path of Transcendental Phenomenology, leading to knowledge in the absolute sense, is "necessarily the path of universal self-knowledge—

first of all monadic and then intermonadic" (Husserl, 1977, p. 156). It is a rational path—knowledge that emerges from a transcendental or pure ego, a person who is open to see what is, just as it is, and to explicate what is in its own terms. A reasoning process follows: "If the only being that can be absolute is the being that can be absolutely given, and if the only being that can be absolutely given is phenomenal being, then only phenomenal being can be absolute being" (Lauer, 1967, p. 151). Phenomenology is the *first* method of knowledge because it begins with "things themselves"; it is also the final court of appeal. Phenomenology, step by step, attempts to eliminate everything that represents a prejudgment, setting aside presuppositions, and reaching a transcendental state of freshness and openness, a readiness to see in an unfettered way, not threatened by the customs, beliefs, and prejudices of normal science, by the habits of the natural world or by knowledge based on unreflected everyday experience.

As far back as I can remember I have sought to know the truth of things through my own intuition and perception, learning from my own direct experience and from awarenesses and reflections that would bring meanings to light. My natural bent was to avoid people who tried to instruct me with their facts and knowings, and to approach things for the first time alone. I have always wanted to encounter life freshly, to allow myself to be immersed in situations in such a way that I could see, really see and know from my own visions and from the images and voices within. When I have been alone I have been free to view openly whatever is before me. I have been able to discern for myself what I am encountering, to explore, to think, to learn, and to know.

The most significant understandings that I have come to I have not achieved from books or from others, but initially, at least, from my own direct perceptions, observations, and intuitions. This has been true in my teaching, my therapy, intimate relationships in my life, my involvement as a parent, and my presence as a person in the everyday world. The most crucial learnings have come from lonely separation from the natural world, from immersions and self-dialogues and from transcendental places of imagination and reflection.

I am very much aligned with a human science that is guided by Epoche, Phenomenological Reduction, Imaginative Variation, and a Synthesis of Meanings and Essences. For me, these have been natural processes through which awareness, understanding, and knowledge are derived. They have evoked in me an unshakable kinship with a philosophy that places ultimate knowledge in the regions and powers of the self.

REFERENCES

Brand, G. (1967). Intentionality, reduction, and intentional analysis in Husserl's later manuscripts. In J. J. Kockelmans (Ed.), *Phenomenology* (pp. 197-217). Garden City, NY: Doubleday.

Descartes, R. (1977). *The essential writings* (J. J. Blom, Trans). New York: Harper & Row.

Descartes, R. (1988). *A discourse on method* (J. Veitch, Trans.). New York: E. P. Dutton. (Original work published 1912)

Farber, M. (1943). *The foundation of phenomenology*. Albany: SUNY Press.

Farber, M. (1967). The ideal of a presuppositionless philosophy. In J. J. Kockelmans (Ed.), *Phenomenology* (pp. 37-57). Garden City, NY: Doubleday.

Fischer, W. F. (1989). An empirical-phenomenological investigation of being anxious. In R. S. Valle & S. Halling (Eds.), *Existential-phenomenological perspectives in psychology* (pp. 127-136). New York: Plenum.

Gurwitsch, A. (1967). On the intentionality of consciousness. In J. J. Kockelmans (Ed.), *Phenomenology* (pp. 118-137). Garden City, NY: Doubleday.

Heidegger, M. (1977). *Basic writings* (D. Krell, Ed.). New York: Harper & Row.

Husserl, E. (1931). *Ideas* (W. R. Boyce Gibson, Trans.). London: George Allen & Unwin.

Husserl, E. (1967). The thesis of the natural standpoint and its suspension. In J. J. Kockelmans (Ed.), *Phenomenology* (pp. 68-79). Garden City, NY: Doubleday.

Husserl, E. (1970). *Logical investigations* (J. N. Findlay, Trans.) (Vol. 1). New York: Humanities Press.

Husserl, E. (1977). *Cartesian meditations: An introduction to metaphysics* (D. Cairns, Trans.). The Hague: Martinus Nijhoff.

Kockelmans, J. J. (Ed.). (1967). *Phenomenology*. Garden City, NY: Doubleday.

Lauer, Q. (1967). On evidence. In J. J. Kockelmans (Ed.), *Phenomenology* (pp. 167-182). Garden City, NY: Doubleday.

Levinas, E. (1967). Intuition of essences. In J. J. Kockelmans (Ed.), *Phenomenology* (pp. 83-105). Garden City, NY: Doubleday.

Miller, I. (1984). *Husserl, perception, and temporal awareness*. Cambridge: MIT Press.

Schmitt, R. (1967). Husserl's transcendental-phenomenological reduction. In J. J. Kockelmans (Ed.), *Phenomenology* (pp. 58-68). Garden City, NY: Doubleday.

Schutz, A. (1967). *A phenomenology of the social world* (G. Walsh & F. Lehnert, Trans.). Evanston, IL: Northwestern University Press.

Smith, Q. (1981, Spring). Husserl's early conception of the triadic structure of the intentional act. *Philosophy Today*, 81-89.

Wertz, F. J. (1985). Methods and findings in a phenomenological psychological study of a complex life event: Being criminally victimized. In A. Giorgi (Ed.), *Phenomenology and psychological research* (pp. 155-216). Pittsburgh: Duquesne University Press.

※※※

3

※※※

PHENOMENOLOGY AND
HUMAN SCIENCE INQUIRY

The task of this chapter is to present theoretical groundings and guidelines for understanding human science from a phenomenological perspective.

EMPIRICAL SCIENCE AND HUMAN SCIENCE

Transcendental science emerged out of a growing discontent with a philosophy of science based exclusively on studies of material things, a science that failed to take into account the experiencing person and the connections between human consciousness and the objects that exist in the material world. In coming to terms with this issue, Descartes (1977) separated mind and body as a way of accentuating the difference between bodies extended in space (objects of empirical investigations) and the mind, which is not material and not extended in space (p. 4). He doubted the reality of external perceptions based solely on studies of bodies in space, and thus recognized that knowledge also emerged from self-evidence. He concluded that what existed in consciousness, whether through intuition or reason, could be depended on unequivocally. The inborn talents of the human person are capable of producing solid and true judgments (p. 22), but material truths are to be held in abeyance and questioned. Thus Descartes (1977) resolved to seek no other science "than that which could be found in myself" (p. 119). With Descartes (1912/1988), philosophy turned toward subjectivity (p. 2). What was said to possess objective reality existed only through representation in the mind; thus Descartes (1912/1988) reasoned that objective reality is in truth subjective reality (p. 249).

From the perspective of transcendental philosophy, all objects of knowledge must conform to experience. Knowledge of objects resides in the subjective sources of the self. Kant (1966) articulated three such sources: sense (phenomena empirically given in perception), imagination (necessary to arrive at a synthesis of knowledge), and apperception (consciousness of the identity of things).

Because all knowledge and experience are connected to phenomena, things in consciousness that appear in the surrounding world, inevitably a unity must exist between ourselves as knowers and the things or objects that we come to know and depend upon.

Descartes's emphasis on knowledge that comes from self-evidence and Kant's transcendental convictions regarding intuitive and a priori sources of knowledge and judgment, markedly contributed to the development of a human science. These contributions made explicit that anything that *is within* us as knowledge such as joy, excitement, or sorrow, actually exists and is unquestionable evidence, in contrast to external things, such as colors, odors, and sounds that exist only in a phenomenal sense.

Brentano (1973) carried forward the perspective of a science of phenomena. He stated without qualification that "experience alone is my teacher" (p. xv). More recently, Schutz (1973), quoting A. N. Whitehead, expressed a similar conviction—that neither common sense nor science can proceed without the strict consideration of what is actual in experience (p. 290).

Brentano (1973) distinguished between the natural sciences, which investigate physical phenomena such as sensations, and the human sciences, which investigate mental phenomena, particularly perception, memory, judgment, and, in general, mental presentations of anything whatsoever. He asserted that, "We have no right to believe that the objects of so-called external perception really exist as they appear to us" (p. 10). Only what we know from internal perception can be counted on as a basis for scientific knowledge.

Husserl (1975) extended Brentano's position regarding the intentional nature of consciousness, the necessity of self-evidence, the value of inner perceptions, and the dependence of knowledge on self-experience. Husserl's quest was a scientific mission, the development of a rigorous science based on philosophy, sound perceptions, ideas, and judgments. For Husserl, as with Descartes and Kant, the "necessary path to knowledge which can be ultimately justified . . . is the path of universal self-knowledge" (1975, p. 39). In this regard, Husserl asserted, "For me the world is nothing other than what I am aware of and what appears valid in my *cognitions* . . . I cannot live, experience, think, value, and act in any world which is not in some sense in me, and derives its meaning and truth from me" (1975, p. 8).

Brentano's insight into the intentional character of consciousness provided the springboard and inspiration for Husserl's extension of a transcendental philosophy.

Husserl's phenomenology is a Transcendental Phenomenology. It emphasizes subjectivity and discovery of the essences of experience and provides a systematic and disciplined methodology for derivation of knowledge (1965, pp. 5-6). Husserl's approach is called "phenomenology" because it utilizes *only* the data available to consciousness—the *appearance* of objects. It is considered "transcendental" because it adheres to what can be discovered through reflection on subjective acts and their objective correlates. It is a "science" because "it affords knowledge that has effectively disposed of all the elements that could render its grasp 'contingent' " (p. 23). It is logical in its assertion that the only thing we know for certain is that which appears before us in consciousness, and that very fact is a guarantee of its objectivity.

In his *Logical Investigations,* Husserl specifies that "logical concepts . . . must have their origin in intuition: they must arise out of ideational intuition founded on certain experiences, and must admit of indefinite reconfirmation" (1970b, pp. 251-252). His emphasis on imagination, ideas, and essences give the human sciences their distinctive character. Further, Husserl asserts that "an epistemological investigation that can seriously claim to be scientific must . . . satisfy the *principle of freedom from suppositions*" (p. 263).

Husserl pointed to a new way of looking at things, a return to things as they actually appear. The new way contrasted sharply with the natural attitude regarding perception, judgment, experience, and thought. It specified that only knowledge that emerged from internal perceptions and internally justified judging satisfied the demands of truth. Harmon (1991), in commenting on these characteristics of human science, emphasized that "science would include more participative kinds of methodologies; it would assume that, whereas we learn certain kinds of things from distancing ourselves from the subject studied, we get another kind of knowledge from intuitively 'becoming one with' the subject. We do not learn about reality from controlled experiments but rather by identifying with the observed" (p. 53).

Although phenomenology is concerned with ideas and essences, there is no denial of the world of nature, the so-called real world. The concept of realism became a major focus of transcendental phenomenology. Realism and objectivity presumably were the province of the natural sciences, yet ultimately the natural sciences operate from ideal principles in that they presuppose that objects that exist in time and space are real, *that they actually exist,* yet there is no evidence that objects are real, apart from our subjective experience of them. Husserl (1965) observed that, "Naturalism recognizes the need of a scientific philosophy, but it is the greatest obstacle because it recognizes as real only the physical. The objectivity which it presupposes is essentially ideal and therefore a contradiction to naturalism's own principles" (p. 9). Husserl concluded that "phenomenology is the 'science of science' since it alone investigates that which all other sciences simply take for granted (or ignore), the very essence of their own objects" (p. 23).

The issue of idealism versus realism is resolved through phenomenological methods in which the meanings and essences of phenomena are derived, not presupposed or assumed. In contrast, the natural sciences "have not in a single instance unravelled for us actual reality, the reality in which we live, move and are" (Husserl, 1965, p. 140). The inadequacy of natural science research is further accentuated in van Kaam's (1969) observation that

> Irrelevant empirical research is produced by the totally detached, abstract, and isolated investigation carried on by the neutral spectator of behavior who is indifferent to the relationship between his abstract game and the life situation. . . . Relevant research is that which explores, describes, and empirically tests human behavior while preserving a "lived" relationship with it in the reality of life. (pp. 26-27)

In phenomenological studies the investigator abstains from making suppositions, focuses on a specific topic freshly and naively, constructs a question or problem to guide the study, and derives findings that will provide the basis for further research and reflection. In phenomenological science a relationship always exists between the external perception of natural objects and internal perceptions, memories, and judgments.

In arriving at essences, Husserl's method involved discovery of knowledge "by reference to the things and facts themselves, as these are given in actual experience and intuition" (1975, p. 6). Husserl was careful to distinguish phenomenologically *objective* reality and *subjective* reality. The objective is the manifest presence of what appears and can be recognized only subjectively by the person who is perceiving it (1970b, p. 314).

The method of reflection that occurs throughout the phenomenological approach provides a logical, systematic, and coherent resource for carrying out the analysis and synthesis needed to arrive at essential descriptions of experience. Husserl (1931) defined *reflection* as a process through which the "stream of experience (*Erlebnis*) with all its manifold events (phases of experience, intentionalities) can be grasped and analyzed in the light of its own evidence" (p. 219). Radical reflection, as viewed by Gurwitsch (1966), begins "by rendering explicit the universal 'presupposition' which underlies all our life" (p. 419).

Following the reflective process, with its disclosure of the actualities and the potentialities of which an object is constituted, the individual constructs a full description of his or her conscious experience. This is called a textural description and includes thoughts, feelings, examples, ideas, situations that portray what comprises an experience.

In the widest sense, evidence is viewed as something that shows itself—something that is there before one. The very act of seeing, just what is there, just as it is, points to further seeing, again and yet again, and to the possibility of confirmation. Husserl (1975) emphasizes that "the confirmation-procedures belong to me as transcendental subjectivity" (p. 23). Confirmation is achieved by repeated looking and viewing while the phenomenon as a whole remains the same.

The challenge of transcendental phenomenology was to develop a method for understanding the objects that appear before us. Such a science requires a return to the self and employment of a self-reflective process that enables the searcher increasingly to know herself or himself within the experience being investigated. For example, as I come to an understanding of the meanings and essences of anger, I also gain knowledge of my own experience of anger. Husserl comments that the world phenomena are initially perceived "through a particular 'manner of appearance,' a particular apperception, open for further reshaping variations . . . through these variations, with certain corrections, there is established the unity of a world having enduring validity as existing, always open to further determinations—including the determination of reality for scientific theory" (1970a, p. 320).

In his writings, Husserl (Carr, 1977) introduced the concept of life-world, the realm of original self-experience that we encounter in an everyday sense. Investigation of the life-world—the way a person lives, creates, and relates in the world—precedes phenomenological reduction. While "science operates with abstractions, the life-world is the concrete fullness from which this abstraction is derived. . . . Science interprets and explains what is given; the life-world is the locus of all givenness" (p. 206).

The experience of the life-world is perceptual experience. Unfortunately, following the position inaugurated by Galileo, the world of ordinary, everyday experience was discarded for an "objectivity" of science that passes as reality (Gurwitsch, 1966, p. 418). Yet every natural science presupposes the existence of a real world and thus departs from its own commitment to objectivity. Husserl's transcendental science offers a carefully developed conceptual model that brings the person into focus as the necessary source for explicating experience and deriving knowledge. Merleau-Ponty (1962) has stated that, "Husserl's essences are destined to bring back all the living relationships of experience, as the fisherman's net draws up from the depths of the ocean quivering fish and seaweed" (p. xv). Essences are brought back into the world and enrich and clarify our knowledge and experience of everyday situations, events, and relationships.

FURTHER DELINEATIONS OF
TRANSCENDENTAL PHENOMENOLOGY

Brentano (1973) divided mental phenomena into three main classes: presentations, which refer to anything whatsoever that appears; judgments of acceptance and rejection; and emotions, referring to love or hate (pp. 197-198). Husserl's (1970b) focus was on pure phenomenology, on essences, on pure consciousness and pure ego (p. 862). No empirical assertions are made and no truths are presupposed or asserted concerning natural realities (1970b, p. 862). Kant (1966) had stated much earlier that to know a thing there must be an intuition through which the object is given to us and a concept by which the object is thought to correspond to the intuition (p. 73). The given object is also a center of transcendental phenomenology; its character must be described rather than explained, the description aiming at an intuitive grasp of the essences embodied within an experience (Husserl, 1965, p. 109).

Husserl's use of *transcendental* is equivalent to the Kantian use of *critical;* transcendental also refers to an opposition to dogmatism of any kind (Landgrebe, 1977, p. 102). Farber (1943) has listed the functions of transcendental phenomenology:

1. It is the *first* method of knowledge because it begins with the things themselves, which are the final court of appeal for all we know. It is a logical approach because it seeks to identify presuppositions and "put them out of play."
2. It is not concerned with matters of fact but seeks to determine meanings.
3. It deals both with real essences and with "possible" essences.
4. It offers direct insight into the essence of things, growing out of the self-givenness of objects and reflective description.
5. It seeks to obtain knowledge through a state of pure subjectivity, while retaining the values of thinking and reflecting. (p. 568)

To summarize, transcendental phenomenology is a scientific study of the appearance of things, of phenomena just as we see them and as they appear to us in consciousness. Any phenomenon represents a suitable starting point for phenomenological reflection. The very appearance of something makes it a phenomenon. The challenge is to explicate the phenomenon in terms of its constituents and possible meanings, thus discerning the features of consciousness and arriving at an understanding of the essences of the experience.

CONSCIOUSNESS

Brentano (1973, pp. 88-98) delineated features of consciousness that guided Husserl's elaboration of phenomenology. He observed that consciousness is intentional; it is directed toward objects; it always contains a content that is intentional. He distinguished between external perception, which relates only to physical phenomena, and internal perceptions of mental phenomena. Phenomena of external perception cannot be proven to be true. The phenomena of inner perception possess *actual existence* as well as intentional existence. There is no act of thinking without an object that is thought; no will without the willing of something; no act of judgment without something being judged; no love without an object of love. In feelings, however, like pain, the consciousness of the pain and the object of pain are fused as one. Otherwise the perceiving act is always directed intentionally toward its object.

Inner perception is dependable and verifiable. According to Brentano (1973) we can always be certain of its veracity because both the presentation and the real object exist within our consciousness (p. 139). Every mental act includes a *presentation,* a cognition, and a feeling, each of which is directed toward a phenomenon.

For the most part, Husserl accepted Brentano's delineation of consciousness. He disagreed, however, that a relationship always exists between perception and reference. In *Logical Investigations* he states:

> If I have an idea of the God Jupiter, this god is my presented object, he is "immanently present" in my act [Husserl substituted *act* for Brentano's *presentation*], he has "mental inexistence" [a term used by Aristotle and later more pointedly by the Scholastics—meaning existing in consciousness]. The intentional experience may be dismembered . . . but the God Jupiter naturally will not be found in it. The "immanent" "mental object" is not part of the real make-up of the experience . . . it does not exist at all. (Husserl, 1970b, p. 558)

From the perspective of phenomenology whether the object actually exists or not makes no difference at all.

Things can emerge in our consciousness in an empty manner and thus our experience moves toward filling them by virtue of looking and looking again, or they can be in thought in a fulfilled manner, the seeing itself bringing about a sense of completion or wholeness of perception. Regardless of how often or from what angles a physical object has been presented to the senses, there is always room for additional meaning (Husserl, 1970b, p. 8).

The phenomenal experience becomes increasingly clarified and expanded in meaning as the phenomenon is considered and reconsidered in reflective processes. Husserl (1975) emphasized that an object has reality in consciousness but that "this reality is reality for me only as long as I believe I can confirm it. By this I mean I must be able to provide useable procedures and other evidences which lead me to the object itself and through which I realize the object as being *truly there*" (p. 23). To illustrate: A friend recently observed that a former colleague whom she had not seen for years was *without a beard* for the first time during the lengthy years of her knowing him. She offered me a vivid and accurate phenomenal description of a well-groomed man. The next day she saw her colleague again and was shocked to discover that *the beard was still there*. She corrected her earlier perception of him as "neat, clean, sharp, and well-groomed" and added "bearded." Unlike the shaggy beard of long ago, it was now "well trimmed and handsome."

The ultimate in understanding experience is a knowledge of essences. In appearance, "stripped of all that is foreign to their appearing," essences can be found (Lauer, 1967, p. 154). The essences of experience are the invariant meanings.

ACT

Husserl (1970b) employed the word *act* rather than *presentation* to refer to experiences of meaning, emphasizing that the meaning of a phenomenon is in the act experience and not in the object. He pointed out that the mere presence of something in consciousness constitutes an act. Objects are perceived but not experienced while sensations are experienced but not perceived, seen, or heard; they are not themselves acts (Husserl, 1970b, p. 567).

There are two sides of every act: Its *quality,* which marks it as a presentation, such as in a judgment, perception, or memory, and its *matter* that lends direction to an object and moves it to present a particular object and no other (Husserl, 1970b, p. 588). Matter includes the features and properties of an object.

Acts are intentional *experiences,* not mental activities (Husserl, 1970b, p. 563). They are either intuitive and full or signitive and empty (1970b, p. 761). The perception in consciousness of the object is no mere intention, "but an act, which may indeed be capable of offering fulfillment to other acts, but which itself requires no further fulfillment" (1970b, p. 712). An object may be perceived from one side and then it may appear near or far away but despite variations and differences "the same object is 'there' . . . a continuous flux of fulfillment or identification, in the steady serialization of the percepts 'pertaining to the same object' " (p. 714). The intuitive act is full when it is validly posited, and signitive when its objective validity has not been determined. In distinguishing the intuitive act that is valid and that which is an illusion, Husserl (1970b) uses the example of a wax figure:

> Wandering about in the Panopticum Waxworks we meet on the stairs a charming lady whom we do not know and who seems to know us, and who is in fact, the well-known joke of the place: we have for a moment been tricked by a waxwork figure. As long as we *are* tricked, we experience a perfectly good percept: we see a lady and not a waxwork figure. When the illusion vanishes, we see exactly the opposite, a waxwork figure that only *represents* a lady. (p. 609)

Through a process of continuing perceiving of and reflecting on acts, we come to know their meaning in our experience and their relationship to ourselves. In each "act of consciousness there are aspects of the object that are not directly intended but which are recognized, either by recall or anticipation, as belonging to the object intended. These constitute its horizons" (Husserl, 1965, p. 150). The act itself "contains its own evidence, its own guarantee of givenness" (Lauer, 1967, p. 151).

PERCEPTION

In phenomenology, perception is regarded as the primary source of knowledge, the source that cannot be doubted. Intentions, united with sensations, make up the full concrete act of perception; the object achieves full-bodied presence (Husserl, 1970b, pp. 608-609). In *Cartesian Meditations,* Husserl (1977) remarked that "Perception floats in the air, so to speak—in the atmosphere of pure phantasizableness. Thus removed from all factualness, it has become the pure 'eidos' perception, whose 'ideal' extension is made up of all ideally possible perceptions" (p. 70). In contrast to the free-floating form of perception that offers an open scanning of the horizon in which entities appear, there is also perceptual attention, the tendency toward sustained perceiving and toward a unity and identity of continual changes that occur in each perceptual act.

With every perception we experience the thing perceived as a one-sided "adumbration" while at the same time apprehending and experiencing the thing as a whole object. Gurwitsch (1966) has observed that, "Throughout the perceptual process, the thing in question appears under a multiplicity of varying aspects which are not only compatible with but also fit into one another" (p. 122). No one or even multiple perceptions ever exhausts the possibilities of knowing and experiencing. New perceptions always hold the possibility of contributing knowledge regarding any object (p. 335).

The perceptions that emerge from angles of looking Husserl calls horizons. In the horizonalization of perceptions every perception counts; every perception adds something important to the experience. The entity or object is never exhausted in properties and meanings. The features of a whole are the horizons, but as with all horizons the moment we single out one meaning the horizon extends again and opens up many other perspectives. Further, along with perceptual acts, as we look and reflect there are acts of memory relevant to a phenomenon that reawaken feelings and images and bring past meanings and qualities into the present. Husserl regards this aspect of temporal awareness as the basic structure of internal time consciousness, its retentive and protentive character (Schutz, 1967, p. 81). Schutz (1967) remarks that protentions into the future are part of every act of memory (p. 57). Miller (1984) points out that the conceptual framework through which one views a phenomenon enables the person to interpret the way things are (p. 83). Merleau-Ponty (1962) adds this vivid description of the process:

> Perception opens a window onto things. This means that it is directed quasi-teleologically towards a *truth in itself* in which the reason underlying all appearances is to be found. The tacit assumption of perception is that every instant experience can be coordinated with that of the previous instant and that of the following and my perspective with that of other consciousnesses, that monadic and intersubjective experience is one unbroken text, that what is now indeterminate for me could become determinate for more complete knowledge. (p. 184)

The whole process takes on the character of wonder as new moments of perception bring to consciousness fresh perspectives, as knowledge is born that unites past, present, and future and that increasingly expands and deepens what something is and means.

Kockelmans (1967) regards perception as the most original act of consciousness, enabling us to express singular judgments that eventuate in universal judgments (p. 27). Perception is the path, the access to truth (Merleau-Ponty, 1962, p. xvi). Perception does not always accurately describe what is present in consciousness. We can easily perceive properties of a thing that it does not possess. Miller (1984) indicates that, "A case of *experience* of misperception is a perceptual experience in the course of which we experience a (purported) object which we continually take to be one and the same while we undergo a 'change of mind' about one or more of its (purported) abiding qualities" (p. 69).

As stated earlier, some perceptions are intuitive, others signitive. Signitive perceptions are empty and must be filled. Schutz (1967) believed that signitive perceptions are the only ways that we can understand the experience of others; they bear directly on our own experiences. He remarks, "I apprehend the lived experiences of another only through my signitive-symbolic representation" (p. 100). He adds,

whenever I have an experience of you, this is still my own experience. However, this experience, while uniquely my own, still has, as its signitively grasped intentional object, a lived experience of yours which you are having at this very moment. In order to observe a lived experience of my own, I must attend to it reflectively. By no means, however, need I attend reflectively to my lived experience of you in order to observe your lived experience. On the contrary, by merely "looking" I can grasp even those of your lived experiences which you have not yet noticed and which are for you still prephenomenal and undifferentiated. This means that, whereas I can observe my own lived experiences only after they are over and done with, I can observe yours as they actually take place. This in turn implies that you and I are in a specific sense "simultaneous," that we "coexist," that our respective streams of consciousness intersect. (p. 102)

In addition to perceptual acts, a primary focus of transcendental philosophy is the act of judgment. Husserl (1977) distinguished two meanings of judgment: the content of judgment, and the epistemic attitude that the person holds toward the judgment, its possibility, probability, or certainty of being true (p. 10).

Husserl (1973) considered prepredicating experiences (the perceptual acts connected with appearances) as the necessary first phase of arriving at judgments. From these, phenomena are increasingly apprehended and lead to ideas and understandings. Husserl concluded that whatever judgments we hold are always dependent on ideas; nowhere in experience do we make judgments apart from ideas.

INTENTIONAL EXPERIENCE

Intentional experiences are acts of consciousness. I perceive a tree. My intentional experience is the combination of the outward appearance of the tree and the tree as contained in my consciousness based on memory, image, and meaning. Memory meanings can be verified by immediate perceptions of what is appearing as tree. Thrusts toward future meanings cannot be validated and yet they exist as genuine possibilities appropriate to my experience of treeness. Thus every experience can be extended in a chain of meanings and essences. Each experience contains openings for further experience. There is no absolute or final reality in experience. Husserl (1973) asserts that:

> Depending on my particular goals, I may have enough of what an experience has already provided me, and then "I just break off" with an "It is enough." However, I can convince myself that no determination is the last, that which has already been experienced always still has, without limit, a horizon of possible experience of the same. (p. 32)

Intentional experience incorporates a real content and an ideal content, in and through which we dwell in thought, perception, memory, judgment, and feeling, in order to comprehend its essences. There is on the one hand "the object itself and the object as meant in this or that manner. On the other hand, we have the object's ideal correlate in the acts of meaning fulfillment which constitute it, the fulfilling sense" (Husserl, 1970b, p. 290). Husserl makes a special point of distinguishing the object *as* it is intended (from one view or angle) and the object *that* is intended (from any angle it is always the same object). These are united through the bestowal of meaning (1970b, p. 608). The treeness of a tree in its essence remains the same whether the tree is viewed from the side, front, or back. From any angle, the tree continues to be experienced intentionally as a whole tree.

Every intentional experience, regardless of how vague or ambiguous it may appear in its origin, intimates something and designates something. Within this framework of meaning, transcendental phenomenology registered a protest against scholasticism and analysis, "Away with empty word analysis! We must question things themselves. Back to experience, to seeing, which alone can give to our words sense and rational justification" (Husserl, 1965, p. 96). Intentional experience *refers* to real entities, objects that actually exist. Frege pointed out long ago that when somebody is thinking about the moon, it is not just the idea of the moon but of an actual, intentional experience in which the moon is the appearing reference or phenomenon (Follesdal, 1982, p. 32).

Every intentional experience is thematic. The interactions of appearing phenomena and acts of consciousness are brought together with at least one theme or reference (Husserl, 1931, p. 304). This is the positing character of intentional experience; at least one thesis is always posited in the concrete makeup of experience.

Another aspect of intentional experience is its *hyletic character*— what the experience includes in the way of sensations and feelings. The *hyle* are experiences that we undergo when we see objects that we perceive or features of objects such as their colors and shapes (Dreyfus & Hall, 1982, p. 39). These contribute to the sense or meaning of any intentional experience.

Meaning is at the heart of a transcendental phenomenology of science. Farber (1943) has pointed out that the expression "The tree is green. . . is alive with a meaning, which is the same in an ideal sense" (p. 223). Such propositions do not have a locus in space and time, they are nonreal (p. 223). Without such features of our mental life, "ordered experience and scientific knowledge would be impossible" (Farber, 1943, p. 223). Farber (1943) has posited three features of meaning situations: (1) acts are meaning-endowing and meaning-fulfilling, which may blend together in fulfillment accomplished through intuition and phantasy; (2) each act in itself contains a meaning; and (3) each act is a reference to an object that is meant (p. 223). Meaning directs a person to gaze at an entity and to be guided by it. Meaning characterizes the rational component of intentional experience.

The object of a conscious act is inseparable from its meaning. Kockelmans (1967, pp. 34-35) characterized the essence of our consciousness as infused with meanings that give objects their particular constitution and that are inseparable from them.

INTERSUBJECTIVE VALIDITY

Husserl's emphasis on monadology as the basis of intentional knowledge did not close out the value of intersubjective knowledge. Such knowledge is needed in coming to know someone or something and in the commitment to copresence and community as a way to verify, accentuate, and extend knowledge and experience. Ego and alter ego are always given and necessary in obtaining various perspectives of what something is and means. For Husserl, the world is a community of persons. Each can experience and know the other, not exactly as one experiences and knows oneself but in the sense of empathy and copresence. In such a process in which I present myself to you and you present yourself to me there is an interchange of perceptions, feelings, ideas, and judgments regarding the nature of reality. A continuing alteration of validity occurs as people articulate and describe their experiences. Reciprocal correcting of reality takes place in social conversations and dialogues. Throughout intersubjective communication, "In reciprocal understanding, my experiences and experiential acquisitions enter into contact with those of others, similar to the contact between individual series of experiences within my experiential life . . . a unification is brought about or at least is certain in advance as possibly attainable by everyone" (Husserl, 1970a, p. 163).

In intersubjective communication the persons are testing out their understanding of each other and their knowledge of something, "sifting out intrusive phrases void of meaning . . . exposing and eliminating errors which here too are possible, as they are in every sphere in which validity counts for something" (Husserl, 1931, p. 256). In the back and forth of social interaction the challenge is to discover what is really true of the phenomena of interpersonal knowledge and experience.

Although the value of intersubjective truth is recognized, Husserl cautions that the beginning point in establishing the truth of things must be individual perception, seeing things as a solitary self. No matter how much one's perceptions depart from others, it is wrong

to jump immediately into transcendental intersubjectivity and to leap over the primal "I," the ego of my epoche, which can never lose its uniqueness and personal indeclinability. . . . Only by starting from the ego and the system of its transcendental functions and accomplishments can we methodically exhibit transcendental intersubjectivity and its transcendental communalization. (Husserl, 1970a, pp. 185-186)

However much we may want to know things with certainty and however much we may count on others' experience to validate our own, in the end only self-evident knowledge enables us to communicate knowingly with each other. The return to the self as the basis for absolute knowledge of the way things are is the first and foremost step. This process of open viewings, of returning to things and being with them, abstaining from the natural attitude, can occur only through my own acts of consciousness, only through my own intentional experience, only through my own direct and open encounter with entities as they appear, and in no other way. Husserl makes self-knowledge the emphatic principle: "In this solitude, I am not a single individual who has somehow willfully cut himself off from the society of mankind. . . . All of mankind, and the whole distinction and ordering of the personal pronouns, has become a phenomenon within my epoche" (1970a, p. 184). And so it is "I," the person among other persons, alone yet inseparable from the community of others, who sees as if for the first time and who reflectively comes to know the meanings that awaken in my consciousness. I am the person who gives existence its essence, the one who returns essence to existential life.

APPLICATIONS TO HUMAN SCIENCE RESEARCH

In reviewing transcendental phenomenology, the following principles, processes, and methods summarize the core facets of human science research.

1. Phenomenology focuses on the appearance of things, a return to things just as they are given, removed from everyday routines and biases, from what we are told is true in nature and in the natural world of everyday living.
2. Phenomenology is concerned with wholeness, with examining entities from many sides, angles, and perspectives until a unified vision of the essences of a phenomenon or experience is achieved.
3. Phenomenology seeks meanings from appearances and arrives at essences through intuition and reflection on conscious acts of experience, leading to ideas, concepts, judgments, and understandings.
4. Phenomenology is committed to descriptions of experiences, not explanations or analyses. Descriptions retain, as close as possible, the

original texture of things, their phenomenal qualities and material properties. Descriptions keep a phenomenon alive, illuminate its presence, accentuate its underlying meanings, enable the phenomenon to linger, retain its spirit, as near to its actual nature as possible. In descriptions one seeks to present in vivid and accurate terms, in complete terms, what appears in consciousness and in direct seeing—images, impressions, verbal pictures, features of heaviness, lightness; sweetness, saltiness; bitterness, sourness; openness, constrictedness; coldness, warmth; roughness, smoothness; sense qualities of sound, touch, sight and taste; and aesthetic properties.

5. Phenomenology is rooted in questions that give a direction and focus to meaning, and in themes that sustain an inquiry, awaken further interest and concern, and account for our passionate involvement with whatever is being experienced. In a phenomenological investigation the researcher has a personal interest in whatever she or he seeks to know; the researcher is intimately connected with the phenomenon. The puzzlement is autobiographical, making memory and history essential dimensions of discovery, in the present and extensions into the future.

6. Subject and object are integrated—what I see is interwoven with how I see it, with whom I see it, and with whom I am. My perception, the thing I perceive, and the experience or act interrelate to make the objective subjective and the subjective objective.

7. At all points in an investigation intersubjective reality is part of the process, yet every perception begins with my own sense of what an issue or object or experience is and means.

8. The data of experience, my own thinking, intuiting, reflecting, and judging are regarded as the primary evidences of scientific investigation.

9. The research question that is the focus of and guides an investigation must be carefully constructed, every word deliberately chosen and ordered in such a way that the primary words appear immediately, capture my attention, and guide and direct me in the phenomenological process of seeing, reflecting, and knowing. Every method relates back to the question, is developed solely to illuminate the question, and provides a portrayal of the phenomenon that is vital, rich, and layered in its textures and meanings.

Intentionality arises first and foremost as a synonym for consciousness itself. We are always intentionally conscious of something; our consciousness points to a direction and has a meaning. As we search into experience, we focus our seeing, our listening, our touching, our thinking on what that experience is in its essences. We examine how it is that that experience is what it is, under what conditions it appears, from what frames of reference, and what its possible meanings are. To be able to deal with questions of love, beauty, anger, suspicion, jealousy, joy, and the like, we first bracket these concerns, shutting out our preconceived biases and judgments, setting aside voices, sounds, and silences that so readily tell us what something is. We describe in detail and fully the whole account of an issue, problem, situation, or experience, using qualities and properties from specific contexts or perspectives, so that the events or experiences take on vivid and essential meanings, a clear portrait of what is. We then reflect on these textural portraits to arrive at their essences, in terms of underlying conditions, precipitating factors, structural determinants. We combine the textural and structural meanings to arrive at the essences of an experience.

Ordinarily the process of searching into the meaning of something involves Epoche to orient us toward looking before judging, and clearing a space within ourselves so that we can actually see what is before us and in us. It involves phenomenological reduction to lead us from complete statements to invariant themes to essential textures and then to imaginative or eidetic reflections based on clues in the textural descriptions. From these steps we arrive at essences connected with universals of temporality, spaciality, bodyhood, materiality, causality, relation to self and others. Then we know for ourselves, in ourselves, from our experiences of others, and from reflections on these experiences, the meanings and essences of entities and experiences in the everyday world.

SUPPOSITIONS IN HUSSERL'S
TRANSCENDENTAL PHENOMENOLOGY

The suppositions that appear in Husserl's (1977) theory of phenomenological reduction, inherent in the first meditation of his *Cartesian Meditations,* are presented below:

1. The first and perhaps most significant presupposition is that one can achieve a pure and absolute transcendental ego, a completely unbiased and presuppositionless state. My own experience in working with

the epoche process is that I can set aside many biases. I can intend an open and fresh approach to my knowledge of something but the problem of language and habit still exist; my own rooted ways of perceiving and knowing still enter in. The value of the epoche principle is that it inspires one to examine biases and enhances one's openness even if a perfect and pure state is not achieved.

2. That self-evidence is apodictic. This assertion presupposes that the perceiving self is an authentic self, that the self is actually present. My experience with extremely disturbed or alienated people and with many people in everyday communications leads to an opposite view. The self is often distorted and disguised. It is presented as a role. An authentic self often does not appear at all. Thus self-evidence may arise from false and inauthentic references, distortions of understanding, and knowledge of experience.

Even if the self is authentically present, a completely free and suppositionless state is itself questionable. Self-evidence, regarded as apodictic, is impossible to validate.

3. That apodictic knowledge exists is a supposition. The "I think, therefore I am" may have certainty at some moment in life but I have experienced times in my life when I could not make the assertion of "I think" or "I am," times of apparent nothingness or confusion where thinking and being itself were remote from my actual experience.

4. That what appears to be appearing is actually appearing. Here there is a supposition that one sees what one sees. Even with many viewings there are many times when one does not see what one sees, that what appears in consciousness is a substitute or distorted perception, a seeming, a disguise, not what is actually there.

5. That the appearing person is actually appearing. Roleplaying, wearing masks, playing a part, and other disguises offer evidence that the person who is appearing is not actually the one who is present. Sometimes a distorted or manufactured image has replaced or is a substitute for a real, authentic person.

Sallis (1982) has made related observations in his analysis of appearances in relationship to identity. He states that to be guided by the thing itself there must be a thing:

> only if the thing is constituted in a fundamental identity with itself, a self-identity . . . one can appeal to the thing itself only if the self of the thing (i.e., what is proper to it, what constitutes its identity) can be delimited in distinction from the *other* of the thing. . . . Thus, beneath the

requirement of rigor there lies a positing of the principle of identity, a positing of the identity of the thing with itself, of its self-identity. (p. 117)

A suppositionless, pure ego state is in itself a supposition. Recognizing the limits of a transcendental phenomenology does not reduce the value of efforts to remove our prejudices, but recognizes and accepts the importance of the epoche process in all searches for and discoveries of knowledge.

APPLICATION TO EDUCATION

In the schools of higher education in which I have been involved in recent years—the Center for Humanistic Studies, the Graduate School of The Union Institute, and the University College of Cape Breton (Family Life Institute)—throughout the educational programs of these schools the emphasis and focus is on individual knowledge, freedom to explore and make choices, and the validity of personal vision, discovery, and self-assessment. First and foremost students have learned to clear, as much as possible, their biases, preconceptions, and prejudgments. They have learned to check into their own conscious awarenesses and attend to whatever is present within.

As a learner, to know *initially* what something is and means, I listen to my inner dialogue, purified as much as possible from other voices, opinions, judgments, and values. This is a challenging task because we are too often taught the reverse in our homes, schools, and society. We are expected to attend to and repeat what other people think, believe, and say regarding what is true.

Ultimately both personal and social knowledge are needed to arrive at valid understandings of reality, but I must first be attuned to my own being, thinking, and choosing before I relate to others' thoughts, understandings, and choices. I must arrive at my own sense of the nature and meaning of something, make my own decision regarding its truth and value before I consider the point of view of others.

Emphasis regarding personal knowledge and self-discovery permeated John Stuart Mill's *On Liberty* (1956), published more than 125 years ago.

Nobody denies that people should be so taught and trained . . . to know and benefit by the ascertained results of human experience. But it is a privilege and proper condition of a human being to use and interpret experience in his own way. It is for him to find out what part of recorded experience is properly applicable to his own circumstances and character. . . . The human faculties of perception, judgment, discriminative feeling, mental activity and even moral preference are exercised . . . only by being used. (pp. 70-71)

This perspective is a dominant focus in my courses and seminars where learners are encouraged to enter into a process of authentic self-presence, thinking, and choosing as a way of discovering and knowing the nature and meaning of significant experiences in identity formation and selfhood. The methods that are central include: growing quiet and listening; coming to an inward clearing; connecting with a dominant question, issue, or concern related to a specific person (including one's own self), or a situation or event; describing the experience; determining the qualities, invariant constituents, and core themes; considering possible meanings; and arriving at an understanding of the essences of the experience.

A typical concern that arises in my seminars is with reference to power. Often the situation focuses on interpersonal life in a relationship or in the family. Questions arise: What is the nature of the power? Who holds the power? How is power communicated? What tactics are used to maintain power? Who makes the critical decisions? How are conflicts resolved? Is power determined by virtue of role or competency? Is the power rational or irrational?

These and similar questions relevant to power are explored descriptively, through examples, and in terms of the learner's self-experience. The challenge is to describe the experience of what power is and how it comes to be—feelings, thoughts, sense responses, how power affects relationship to self and others. In the process of developing full descriptions of their experience of power in interpersonal relationships and in the family, learners discover what power is and means, how it shows itself in consciousness, and how it relates to personality and identity. In closing this section, I offer an example of a descriptive account of one student's depiction of power and authority in the family.

My father was the power and authority in my family. He married when he was young and had set ideas on how to discipline. He was quite arbitrary, and always had the first and last word. This control still exists but since he is involved in work and sports, I have replaced him to a degree in regard to the power and authority within our family framework . . . as for my mother, I have always had my own way in my dealings with her.

I realized at an early age that I could easily boss around my younger brother and sister. This trait still exists within me and I still have control over them, but to a lesser degree. I was 8 years old when my brother was born and from the beginning I groomed my brother to be utterly dependent on me. I took him everywhere, helped him with school and sports, and bought him whatever he liked. In return he idolized me and strived for my approval.

Foote and Cottrell in their book *Identity and Interpersonal Competence* define power as the "ability to produce intended effects." Unconsciously as a child I did this to my brother and I like the feeling of him depending on me. It made me feel stronger than I actually was, and gave him security. This power relationship was definitely negative but it seemed to fulfill a need within us. It wasn't until I went to college, that we both learned to live without this dependency. Now my brother looks to me for approval but I would never be permitted to get away with exercising the previous degree of power over him.

I have the power in our family and I do realize that it is negative. My parents depend on me far too much, and I feel this is because I am the oldest. Next year I will move away and I hope that this will lead to their own development of their personal positive power.

As for my personal power, I am a decision-maker and like to hold responsibility and dominate—not over others as much as to be pleased with myself. Perhaps, as the oldest child, I do consider power an important thing in life and strive to retain it.

From this report it is possible to develop a descriptive portrait of what power means. For Cathy, it is the ability to influence others, to obtain intended effects, to exert control over others while also pleasing herself. It involves dominating others, making decisions, holding responsibility. Power, as developed by Cathy, is the power of the role, the oldest child, consciously and deliberately creating dependencies in order to feel her strength, in order to teach others, take care of them, and help them feel secure. Through these ways she evokes in other family members the need for her opinions and approval. Cathy views these qualities as forms of negative power and would prefer to move toward a personal power that focuses on fulfillment of self-interests, yet there remains in her the need to retain her power over others and to some degree over their lives.

CONCLUDING COMMENTS

As I come to a closing place in this reflective and meditative journey I am alive with images and ideas, struck with the wonder of passionately discovering that the only way I can truly come to know things and people is to go out to them, to return again and again to them, to immerse myself completely in what is there before me, look, see, listen, hear, touch, from many angles and perspectives and vantage points, each time freshly so that there will be continual openings and learnings that will connect with each other and with prior perceptions, understandings, and future possibilities. In other words, I must immerse myself totally and completely in my world, take in what is offered without bias or prejudgment. I must pause and consider what my own life is and means, in conscious awareness, in thought, in reflections. I enter into my own conscious reflections and meditations, open and extend my perceptions of life and reach deeper meanings and essences. This connectedness between what is out there, in its appearance and reality, and what is within me in reflective thought and awareness, is in truth a wondrous gift of being human. But knowledge does not end with moments of connectedness, understanding, and meaning. Such journeys open vistas to new journeys for uncovering meaning, truth, and essence—journeys within journeys, within journeys. This is perhaps the most telling reality of all, that each stopping place is but a pause in arriving at knowledge. Satisfying as it is, it is but the inspiration for a new beginning. Knowledge of appearances and reasoned inquiry are not the end of knowing. No scientific discovery is ever complete. No experience is every finished or exhausted. New and fresh meanings are forever in the world and in us. When the connection is made and the striving comes alive again, the process begins once more. There is no limit to our understanding or sense of fulfillment, no limit to our knowledge or experience of any idea, thing, or person. We need only to come to life again regarding some puzzlement and everything crystallizes in and through and beyond it. The whole process of being within something, being within ourselves, being within others, and correlating these outer and inner experiences and meanings is infinite, endless, eternal. This is the beauty of knowledge and discovery. It keeps us forever awake, alive, and connected with what is and with what matters in life.

66 PHENOMENOLOGICAL RESEARCH METHODS

REFERENCES

Brentano, F. (1973). *Psychology from an empirical standpoint* (A. C. Rancurello, D. B. Terrell, & L. L. McAllister, Trans.). New York: Humanities Press.

Carr, D. (1977). Husserl's problematic concept of the life-world. In F. Elliston & P. McCormick (Eds.), *Husserl expositions and appraisals* (pp. 202-212). Notre Dame, IN: University of Notre Dame Press.

Descartes, R. (1988). *A discourse on method* (J. Veitch, Trans.). New York: E. P. Dutton. (Original work published 1912)

Descartes, R. (1977). *The essential writings* (J. Blom, Ed.). New York: Harper & Row.

Dreyfus, H. L., & Hall, H. (1982). *Husserl, intentionality and cognitive science.* Cambridge: MIT Press.

Farber, M. (1943). *The foundation of phenomenology.* Albany: SUNY Press.

Follesdal, D. (1982). Brentano and Husserl on intention objects and perception. In H. L. Dreyfus & H. Hall (Eds.), *Husserl, intentionality, and cognitive science* (pp. 31-41). Cambridge: MIT Press.

Foote, N. N., & Cottrell, L. S. (1955). *Identity and interpersonal competence.* Chicago: University of Chicago Press.

Gurwitsch, A. (1966). *Studies in phenomenology and psychology.* Evanston, IL: Northwestern University Press.

Harmon, W. W. (1991). On the shape of a new science. *ICIS Forum, 21*(1), 50-55.

Husserl, E. (1931). *Ideas* (W. R. Boyce Gibson, Trans.). London: George Allen & Unwin.

Husserl, E. (1965). *Phenomenology and the crisis of philosophy* (Q. Lauer, Trans.). New York: Harper & Row.

Husserl E. (1970a). *The crisis of European sciences and transcendental phenomenology: An introduction to phenomenological philosophy* (D. Carr, Trans.). Evanston, IL: Northwestern University Press.

Husserl, E. (1970b). *Logical investigations* (Vols. 1 & 2) (J. N. Findlay, Trans.). New York: Humanities Press.

Husserl, E. (1973). *Experience and judgment* (J. S. Churchill & K. Ameriks, Trans.). Evanston, IL: Northwestern University Press.

Husserl, E. (1975). *The Paris lectures* (P. Koestenbaum, Trans.) (2nd ed.). The Hague: Martinus Nijhoff.

Husserl, E. (1977). *Cartesian meditations: An introduction to metaphysics* (D. Cairns, Trans.). The Hague: Martinus Nijhoff.

Kant, I. (1966). *Critique of pure reason.* Garden City, NY: Doubleday.

Kockelmans, J. J. (1967). What is phenomenology? In *Phenomenology* (pp. 24-36). Garden City, NY: Doubleday.

Landgrebe, L. (1977). Phenomenology as transcendental theory of history. In F. Elliston & P. McCormick (Eds.), *Husserl expositions and appraisals* (pp. 101-113). Notre Dame, IN: University of Notre Dame Press.

Lauer, Q. (1967). On evidence. In J. J. Kockelmans (Ed.), *Phenomenology* (pp. 150-157). Garden City, NY: Doubleday.

Merleau-Ponty, M. (1962). *Phenomenology of perception* (C. Smith, Trans.). Boston: Routledge & Kegan Paul.

Mill, J. S. (1956). *On liberty.* Indianapolis: Bobbs-Merrill.

Miller, I. (1984). *Husserl, perceptions, and temporal awareness.* Cambridge: MIT Press.

Sallis, J. (1982). The identities of the things themselves. *Research In Phenomenology, XII,* 113-126.

Schutz, A. (1967). *A phenomenology of the social world* (G. Walsh & F. Lehnert, Trans.). Evanston, IL: Northwestern University Press.

Schutz, A. (1973). A common sense and scientific interpretation of human action. In R. Zaner & D. Ihde (Eds.), *Phenomenology and existentialism.* New York: G. P. Putnam.

van Kaam, A. (1969). *Existential foundations of psychology.* Garden City, NY: Doubleday.

INTENTIONALITY, NOEMA,
AND NOESIS

Perhaps no concepts in transcendental phenomenology are more fraught with complexity than those of intentionality, noema, and noesis. At the same time, none are more critical to an understanding of human science and in searches for knowledge in research investigations. The running stream of argumentation recreates the old-time conflicts of the analytic versus transcendental philosophers: Does language precede meaning or does meaning precede language? Does perceptual experience determine meaning or is meaning an outcome of concepts and judgments? Is meaning embedded in experience itself or is it an outgrowth of reflection and afterthought? There is general agreement that meaning is at the heart of perceiving, remembering, judging, feeling, and thinking; agreement too that, in perceiving, one is perceiving something (whether actually existing or not); one is remembering something, judging something, feeling something, thinking something, whether the something is real or not. There is also agreement that intentionality directs consciousness *toward* something (real or imaginary, actual or nonexistent); that the noema gives consciousness its direction toward specific objects. The noema ascribes meaning to what one sees, touches, thinks, or feels. All experience holds within it essential meanings.

My objective in this chapter is to explore intentionality as embodied in the concepts of noema and noesis, and move forward in practical ways toward a basic comprehension and applications of these concepts.

NOEMA AND NOESIS

Husserl (1931) introduced concepts of noesis and noema in *Ideas*, stating that the noeses constitute the mind and spirit, and awaken us to the meaning or sense of whatever is in perception, memory, judgment, thinking, and feeling (p. 249). The noetic side refers to the psychical in contrast to the sensory side, which refers to the physical. Husserl considered the word *psychical* a misleading term and preferred using the direct language of thinking, reflecting, feeling, remembering, and judging. In intentional experience there is a material side and a noetic or ideal side.

The noeses bring into being the consciousness of something. In and through the noeses objects appear, shine forth, and are "rationally" determined (1931, p. 251).

The noesis refers to the act of perceiving, feeling, thinking, remembering, or judging—all of which are embedded with meanings that are concealed and hidden from consciousness. The meanings must be recognized and drawn out.

The other central concept of intentionality is that of noema. The noema corresponds at all points to the noesis. Wherever a noesis exists it is always directly related to a noema. The noema, in perception, is its perceptual meaning or the perceived as such; in recollection, the remembered as such; in judging, the judged as such (Husserl, 1931, p. 258). Ihde (1977) offers this distinction: noema is *that* which is experienced, the what of experience, the object-correlate. Noesis is the way in which the what is experienced, the experiencing or act of experiencing, the subject-correlate (p. 43).

In perception, certain questions stand out: "What is the 'perceived as such'?" (Husserl, 1931, p. 260). What are the essential features or phases of perceptual experience that constitute the essence of an entity? Husserl suggests, "We win the reply to our question as we wait, in pure surrender, on what is actually *given*. We can then describe 'that which appears as such' faithfully and in the light of perfect self-evidence" (p. 260).

Husserl differentiates between the intentional object, the object that appears in consciousness and the actual object, between the ideal in perception and the real as it is perceived in accordance with the everyday natural attitude. He remarks,

> The *tree plain and simple,* the thing in nature, is as different as it can be from this *perceived tree as such,* which as perceptual meaning belongs to the perception, and that inseparably. The tree plain and simple can burn away, resolve itself into its chemical elements, and so forth. But the meaning of *this* perception, something that belongs necessarily to its essence—cannot burn away; it has no chemical elements, no forces, no real properties. (Husserl, 1931, p. 260)

The noesis and noema refer to meanings. When we look at something what we see intuitively constitutes its meaning. When we reflect upon something and arrive at its essence, we have discovered another major component of meaning. To the extent that the perceptual meaning of an object refers to a reality, we are describing a real thing. The description of a thing incorporates its meaning. Thus the Husserlian "back to things themselves" is a way of emphasizing knowledge that is rooted in meanings rather than in an analysis of physical objects.

In reflecting on what one has "seen" and described, one is coming to an understanding of meanings that have been concealed. What one sees, each time one looks at something or judges something, is its noema, the perceived as such or the judged as such. Inherent in this process are many meanings, the noemata that connect or synthesize in such a way that one comes to know not only the parts or aspects of a thing but also its unity or wholeness. Husserl calls the partial views of a whole entity the noematic phases. The phases correspond to one another, add layers of meaning to each other, correlate with each other and form a comprehensive meaning of the wholeness of a thing. The challenge in this process of looking and reflecting, looking and reflecting again, is to obtain true, accurate, and complete descriptions, both in the preliminary phases of viewing something, of letting it linger before one, and in the noetic phases of reflecting on the experience, to discover its hidden meanings. Husserl (1931) emphasizes the significance of description: "The decisive factor lies before all in the absolutely faithful description of that which lies before one in phenomenological purity, and in keeping at a distance all interpretations that transcend the given" (p. 262). Only what is *given* bears emphasis and repetition, only what the experience intends is described; only what *presents* itself as we perceive, think or feel.

With reference to the noematic, the meaning is precisely what is given in the act of perceiving, remembering, or judging, just what is *intended*, what *appears*, what is *presented*; only that is the focus and emphasis of the noematic phases that are always involved in understanding what something is and means. Internal perception, appearance, and experience work together to capture the meaning of the perceived as such.

What "is immediately and directly presented to consciousness," states Edie (1967), "is surrounded by and *given with* a ground of interlocking 'horizons' which constitute the 'sense' or structure of the perceptual experience . . . *that which* is experienced—the very contact with the 'thing itself'—and not an intellectual or conceptual construction" (pp. 243-244).

We must not lose sight of the fact that a person is *present* in perception, someone who perceives what is given, enters into an encounter with it, a person who may be awakened to memory, wish, imagination, or judgment, a person relating to the "thing itself" and the "thing as a whole." Husserl (1931) brings this meaning intimately to our attention: "the real object is the thing out there. We see it, we face it, we have turned our eyes towards it and fixed them upon it, and as we find it there in space over against us, so we describe it and make our statements concerning it" (p. 264).

Whether one is perceiving, remembering, judging, or imagining, there are common threads in one's intentional experience of something. At the same time, there are unique meanings in each of these modes or acts of experience.

Inevitably when one perceives or imagines or judges something, shifts are bound to occur as one looks from a different frame of reference, mood, or internal locus. When one looks with confidence, what one sees will be radically different than when one looks with doubt. What at first appears plain and simple, suddenly becomes filled with ambiguity, and we wonder if

we have not been made victims of a mere "illusion." . . . The thing "suggests" a man. Then a contrary suggestion sets in: it might be a moving tree, which in the gloom of the wood resembles a man in motion. But the "weight" of the one "possibly" is now considerably reinforced, and we decide in favour perhaps, definitely presuming that "it was surely a tree." (Husserl, 1931, p. 297-298)

With every intentional object that appears in imperfect givenness, there is the ideal possibility of its perfection, of its reaching a more definite and dependable shape, a more perfect intuition. Inadequate descriptions or unfinished acts of consciousness inspire continued looking and reflecting, continued consideration of other possible visions, understandings, judgments, of what a thing truly is. Husserl (1931) emphasizes that:

> No thing-perception is terminal and conclusive; space always remains for new perceptions which would . . . fill in the perceptual gaps . . . *every* perception and perceptual manifold is capable of being extended; the process is thus endless; accordingly no intuitive apprehension of the essence of the Thing can be so complete that a further perception could not bring it something noematically new. (p. 414)

In the process of recalling an experience, for example, shadings are clarified; details are added; refinements bring new voices, sounds, and visions. This is a natural process as we extend and correct our perceptions, memories, and judgments, as we elucidate our experience. The reflective process makes possible deeper exploration of the intentional structures of noesis and noema. What is called for is a glancing ray of the ego that shifts from the inward focus of perception to the magnetism of memory, to the glory of imagination, to the reasonable assertions of judgment, "wandering here and there, passes on to memories . . . or into worlds of fancy" (Husserl, 1931, p. 268). In the search, deeper and deeper layers of meaning unfold; qualities and constituents of an experience linger and endure. The material elements of phenomena undergo (through the noetic phases) " 'formal shapings' and 'gifts of meaning,' which we grasp, in reflexion, upon and with the material elements" (1931, p. 284). Noematic elements fall back on the noetic phases; the noetic phases return to noematic features; a rhythm is established. Richer and more extended descriptions of an experience are realized. The shift from a phenomenon and our perception of it to reflective examination of our conscious experience of it occurs throughout a phenomenological study.

Each time new components of an experience emerge, different acts of consciousness direct us to new understandings of the experience. The intentional experience becomes increasingly articulated in its features and qualities and as a whole as we consider it again and again. Description of the noematic qualities is the objective component and always relates to a subjective consciousness, the noesis. A noetic description is always subjective and connects with the object as perceived. Husserl (1931) exclaims,

> a fully *dependable content* is marked off *in every noema*. Every consciousness has its "what" and "its" objective; it is evident that in the case of every such consciousness we must be able as a matter of principle to carry out a noematic description of this same objective "exactly as it is meant." (p. 364)

Each act of consciousness intends some object or entity, "not with an undifferentiated blankness, but . . . with a describable *structure of multiplicities,* a structure having a *quite definite* noetic-noematic composition" (Husserl, 1977, p. 40).

Of course in the back and forth from appearance, to consciousness, to experience, a person is very much present. Prior to any consciousness or directedness toward phenomena or intentional experience there is an existing individual. Presumably this person has set aside biases and has come to a place of readiness to gaze on whatever appears and to remain with that phenomenon until it is understood, until a perceptual closure is realized. Throughout, whether in noematic phases or in noetic unfoldings, a person who lives in the everyday world exists as a self, both independent from and in communion with other selves. Ihde (1977) has emphasized that the phenomenological process begins a self, who consciously thinks, remembers, perceives, imagines, and judges and who by virtue of the noema is directed toward certain things (actual or nonexistent), a person who moves between appearance and reflection. The unity of person and object in the conscious act of perception is ineradicable. At any moment a striking memory or a phenomenon or marked attraction may captivate the person.

I have been emphasizing the intimate relationship between noesis and noema. In spite of this continuing correlation it is possible within our experience to focus outwardly and gaze upon the phenomenon as such, describe the phenomenon just as it appears before us, and continue to look and focus until we have incorporated many of its dimensions. In this process our attention has been external. The noema directs us to an intuitive explication of the phenomenon in a prereflective manner. We look and describe; we look again and describe, until there is a sense of having fulfilled our intention, of having arrived at a breaking off point, of having a sense of completion or closure, of really knowing what is there before us.

Intriguing questions awaken in reviewing the process: Does our consciousness direct us via the noema to the phenomenon or does the phenomenon itself call out to us? Certainly when the entity is another person it is clear that it may happen either way. I may be called or I may do the calling. Or, there may be a mutual, immediate attraction. But what about a tree, a leaf, a stone, the river or mountain stream, a cloud? Is there not something in the way of each of these entities that gazes upon us while we gaze upon it? What draws us to something? Is it the noema that compels us toward one phenomenon rather than another, as Husserl claims? Or, is there something inherent in the nature of all things, in the way of mutual callings, or attractions? How is it that I am inclined toward one kind of rock rather than another? Is it truly something in me that propels me in one direction rather than another?

Something in a phenomenon may draw me, like a magnet, toward it. Something in me may compel me toward some specific person or thing. Or, some mutual attraction or instant harmony with others may conspire toward our joining or connecting with one another. In any case when the gaze is outward toward something, there is in that moment a noematic meaning and an intuition that in the very first vision or touch or fragrance fills the phenomenon, to some degree, fills the empty presence with sense and meaning.

It is also possible to look inwardly, to examine directly and deliberately one's conscious experience of something (as I have just demonstrated in my own reflections on the meaning of noema, on the nature of external perception, and on the way of entities and persons). The experience itself of perceiving, remembering, imagining, judging, is always with reference to something and is always open to my consideration, to my reflection. As I look internally, I am more and more able to describe the different possibilities and meanings inherent in my act of consciousness, until I feel satisfied that I have arrived at a comprehensive and integral meaning that embraces the whole of my experience.

Ultimately, to arrive at the essences of a phenomenon, I must unify the noema and the noesis, even when my focus is basically external or basically internal. The interweaving, the rhythms of noema-noesis, creates a harmony and an integral understanding of an experience.

In viewing intentionality a number of additional ideas stand out as primary themes. These are discussed in the sections that follow.

IDENTITY AND TEMPORALITY

How identity is achieved and how it relates to temporality has been a continuing theme in transcendental phenomenology. Gurwitsch (1966) extensively examined these concepts from philosophical perspectives and came to believe that the noema-noesis process is an answer to the problem of how identical and identifiable objects remain the same and yet undergo temporal variations (pp. 131-132). In this process there is "the act as a real event in psychical life, happening at a certain moment in phenomenal time, lasting, disappearing, and, when it has disappeared, never returning" (p. 132), and there is also what stands before the perceiving subject's mind. How is it then that a phenomenon continues to be the same in perception, continues to be identified, as such, no matter how many times or how sharply we move away from it? The identity remains whether the entity comes into existence through perception, imagination, recollection, or desire. It is still the same entity every time it appears.

At every moment of perception we find variations in what we perceive, a continual passing away of one thing and the appearance of another thing, yet each time something essential is retained and carried forward into the next moment. Gurwitsch (1966) views identity and temporality as related to each other, like the twin correlations of noema and noesis (pp. 136-137). In arriving at this position Gurwitsch has taken into account Hume's and Husserl's constructions, concluding that Hume failed adequately to consider the nature and meaning of identity, as influenced by and related to temporality. For Hume, only temporality is needed to account for the sameness of the successive appearances of an object. He observed that the resemblance among sense data in different viewings of an entity enables the mind to pass smoothly and easily from one perception to another

> that it is scarcely aware of the transition. This resemblance puts the mind
> in a state similar to that in which it is when it surveys, without interruption,
> an unchangeable object for some time; this later state gives rise to the idea

of identity . . . the mind mistakes similarity for identity. (Gurwitsch, 1967, p. 121)

This means that no matter how many times one opens and closes one's eyes, for example in viewing a particular lamp, although there are variations in the perceiving, one will see that same lamp each time. According to Hume, each time the mind must recall previous perceptions, holding onto what stands out as core and eliminating details that would present the object differently. Because identity consists in the illusion of holding the resembling items to be a single reality, all interfering details disappear (Gurwitsch, 1966, p. 122). Via imagination one perceives the lamp to be a single, identical object each time. Imagination devises "the further fiction of a 'continued existence' ascribed to the 'broken and interrupted' appearances" (Gurwitsch, 1966, p. 128).

In this view, identity and temporality are working against each other. Temporality destroys identity while giving the illusion that something that returns to consciousness is identifiable as that same something that has appeared previously. In referring to Hume's thesis, Gurwitsch (1967) comments, "As long as we are inattentive enough, we may believe in identity, although in reality there is merely a succession of resembling items" (p. 124). Nonetheless, in everyday experience, we are able to verify that what I saw yesterday, I see today. Thus, in experience, identity and temporality come together.

Husserl solved the problem by correlating identity with temporality, utilizing his theory of intentionality, and particularly, the noema-noesis process (Gurwitsch, 1967, p. 127). The object in a multiplicity of perceptions shows itself as the same object; whatever series of perceptions may succeed one another. From different perspectives the same object continues to appear in consciousness. My experience of a house is still that of a house though I may view it differently in its noematic phases, from front to side to back. Amplifying this point, Gurwitsch (1967) observes that "these perceptions enter into a synthesis of identification with one another, and it is by, and in, this synthesis and the parallel synthesis among the corresponding noemata, that what appears successively constitutes itself, for consciousness, into this real thing which it is, one and identical" (p. 129). With each passing perception, I view and describe a multiplicity of qualities in a thing "which, by virtue of its essential nature, pertains to just *this* identical cogitatum" (Husserl, 1977, p. 40).

Each noematic perception enters and departs, with its temporal phases; the phases connect so that although there are changing appearances a unity of phases occurs, a synthesis that marks the identity of a phenomenon. The multiple modes of appearance become constituted so that one identical phenomenon continues to appear (Husserl, 1977, p. 42). The identified object is intentional in consciousness. The same identical phenomenon can appear in successive modes of consciousness, in memory, perception, or imagination. Husserl (1977) comments that "a unitary consciousness *embracing* these separated processes, gives rise to the consciousness of identity and thereby makes any knowing of identity possible. . . . The *fundamental form* of this universal synthesis, the form that makes all other syntheses of consciousness possible, is the all-embracing *consciousness of internal time*" (pp. 42-43).

Duration is also an essential factor in understanding how the identification of objects is possible. There is an "incessant transformation of every actual now" into a "having just been an actual now . . . the present moment ceasing to be present, is yet retained in 'primary memory' and takes the form of 'having just been present' " (Gurwitsch, 1967, p. 132). The incessant variations constitute the "stream-character of consciousness" (p. 133).

SIGNITIVE AND INTUITIVE

Another component of transcendental phenomenology is accentuated in the distinction between the two types of intention: the signitive intention, which is "empty" and points to something that lies beyond itself, and the intuitive intention, which points to something directly and fulfills it to some degree. Intuitive intention hits the target and makes possible apprehension of the intentional object in some feature or quality and ultimately as a whole, but signitive intention refers to something in its absence. It announces something that has the possibility of appearing or that exists within the intuitive. In *Logical Investigations,* Husserl (1970) states that signitive acts constitute the lowest in the manner in which objects are presented; "they possess no fullness whatever" (p. 761). The signitive makes its appearance and in doing so points to and may trigger an expression that has been just out of awareness, or it may connect with an intuitive grasp of something and thus bring the intuitive into expression.

The "filling out" of intentional experience is an important factor in understanding the noema and noesis. Husserl (1931) stresses that fullness of meaning is not the only concern; the mode of filling out is itself a requisite to its meaning. He emphasizes that, "One mode of experiencing the meaning is the *'intuitive,'* whereby we are made aware of the 'meant object as such' through direct mental vision" (p. 380). Thus the perceptual intuition is a fulfilling act. Dreyfus and Hall (1982) also comment on this, specifying: (1) that it fulfills a certain signifying intention and (2) it must be sensuously given for "a signitive intention merely points to its object, an intuitive intention gives it 'presence' " (p. 103). The signifying act intends for its object to have certain characteristics that the signification enables, recognizes, and anticipates while the intuitive act determines its object.

TEXTURE AND STRUCTURE

In considering description as the primary method of presenting intentional experience, certain basic questions arise: What is the nature of the phenomenon? What are its qualities? What appears at different times and under varying conditions? The challenge of description is to determine the textural components of experience, the "what" of the appearing phenomenon. Ihde (1977) has stated that, *"every experiencing has its reference or direction towards what is experienced and, contrarily, every experienced phenomenon refers to or reflects a mode of experiencing to which it is present"* (pp. 42-43). It is this "what" that must be explicated texturally in order to arrive at the noematic phases and the full noema as it is given. In the textural description of an experience nothing is omitted; every dimension or phase is granted equal attention and is included. In transcendental phenomenology one begins with the bracketing of a phenomenon, the residual of what remains of the natural world, following the Epoche. It is this, within brackets, that is texturally described from many sides, angles, and views, until a sense of fulfillment is reached. From an extensive description of the textures of what appears and is given, one is able to describe *how* the phenomenon is experienced. This means turning one's focal attention to the conditions that precipitate the textural qualities, the feelings, sense experiences, and thoughts, the structures that underlie textures and are intimately bound within them. Keen (1975) defines *structures* as "that order embedded in everyday experience which can be grasped only through reflection" (p. 46). Thus, although textural description of the noematic correlate and of the whole noema is intuitive and prereflective, structural description involves conscious acts of thinking and judging, imagining, and recollecting, in order to arrive at core structural meanings. Structures underlie textures and are inherent in them. Keen (1975) comments that, "It is not possible to describe texture without implicit notions of structure" (p. 58). Texture and structure are in continual relationship. In the process of explicating intentional experience one moves from that which is experienced and described in concrete and full terms, the "what" of the experience, "towards its reflexive reference in the 'how' of the experience" (Ihde, 1977, p. 50).

The relationship of texture and structure is not that of object and subject or concrete and abstract but of the appearance and the hidden coming together to create a fullness in understanding the essences of a phenomenon or experience. Keen (1975) advises that, "The interlocking of texture and structure does not preclude the possibility of focusing on one or the other at any given stage of phenomenological work" (p. 59).

PERCEPTION OR CONCEPTION?

A major disagreement regarding the nature of the noema has been the focus of considerable attention in transcendental philosophy; specifically what Husserl meant or did not mean. One assertion is that a noema is a concept, an abstract entity that is completely divorced from the object intended; the opposite position is that a noema is a percept that is intimately bound up with the object itself. Perception is a concept; perceptual experience is not. There is agreement that the noema has two components: one *common* to all acts regardless of their thetic character (whether an act is that of perceiving, remembering, judging, and so forth) and one which is *different* in acts of different thetic characters (Follesdal, 1982, p. 75). The issue becomes pronounced in terms of the actuality of the relationship between the noema and the intended object. It is not a matter of whether the noema directs perception or memory or judgment but the connection between noema and entity. Husserl (1970) states that, "The object is not actually given, wholly and entirely as that which it itself is. It is only given 'from the front,' only perspectivally foreshortened and projected" (p. 712). He adds, "We must, however, note that the object, as it is *in itself* . . . is *not wholly different* from the object realized, however imperfectly, in the percept" (p. 713). And: "In one percept the object appears from this side . . . now it appears close, now at a distance etc. In each percept, despite these differences, one and the same object is 'there,' in each it is intended in the complete range of its familiar and of its perceptually present properties" (p. 714). To repeat, "the object, as it is *in itself*—in the only sense relevant and understandable . . . is *not wholly* different from the object realized, however imperfectly, in the percept" (Husserl, 1970, p. 713).

Holmes (1975) offers a similar perspective, concluding that object and noema are bound together. He suggests three components of the noema: "(a) the intentional object, (b) the noematic senses; and (c) the particular manner of their being given" (p. 153). The main point is that the noema and the intended object are inseparable parts of the intentional experience, that what one sees intentionally bears an immediate relationship to what actually appears.

Solomon (1977) is also convinced that, "Husserl's concept of the noema is an attempt to establish a common ground for both the problems of perception and the foundations of necessary truths and judgments" (p. 169). Solomon proposes that both perception and judgment enter into intentional experience and that an absurdity occurs when it is suggested that the perceived as such is not itself perceived for all experience requires meaning, not as an after-the-fact luxury in reflective judgments but in order for it to be an experience *of* anything (pp. 175-179).

Throughout our initial efforts to know something, there is a constant flow of percept and concept; the senses are directly involved in the noematic phases, as are ideas. We perceive and conceptualize in every situation where the aim is to describe phenomena in a clear and full sense. We see perhaps more strikingly, in a more attentive way, in our initial intuition or in the signification of something that exists as possibility. Thus spontaneous encounters with phenomena enable fresh points of view that occur largely through perceptions. As we look again and again, there is movement from a prereflective givenness to a reflective focus. Attention moves from the internal perception that is spontaneous and immediate in conscious knowing of the intended object to an external reflective process that includes selection, judgment, and choice. In the noema-noesis relationship there is a shift to internal consciousness where ideas and judgments are more fully the focus of our attention. Through perceptions we fulfill the requirements of bracketing and phenomenological reduction and are able to develop full textural descriptions. As the reflective process becomes more pronounced and needed, the focus of attention shifts from percept to concept, from texture to structure, from what is immediate to possible meanings. In the search there is a constant interplay of the real and the ideal, a definite movement toward ideas, understandings, and judgments. Perceptions bring textural descriptions to life, in explicating the "what" of our experience; whereas reflection and conceptualization ferret out undisclosed meanings. Thus both percept and concept enter into all noematic and noetic phases; first one prominently and then the other, with the ultimate challenge being an integration of the perceptual and the cognitive in order to arrive at essential meanings.

Intentionality offers a freedom to perceive and view things just as they appear, permits them to be, and makes possible the recognition, elucidation, and synthesis of what appears. Essence and existence blend to make for a continual enriching and extending of human knowledge and a continuing dialogue and communion between persons, conscious experiences, and things.

THE EXPERIENCE OF TIME

From these studies, and an incident that bounded me absolutely to each hour of the clock, I found myself spontaneously entering into a phenomenological description of my experience of time, its entrance, endurance, and passing, its noematic and noetic ways, in my perceptions, memories, judgments, feelings, aspirations. I offer the following expression as a reflection of the personal meaning of time engendered by this study of intentionality, noema and noesis, as the outcome of bracketing and as the explication of my experience of time.

Many times in my life, time has held the key to being, to meaning, to emergence, to anguish and misery.

I can remember moments that I wanted to hold onto and savor and protect, unfoldings that were just beginning or had not reached a peak of fulfillment. Time rushed in and the growing stopped; moments of leaving or being left awakened deep feelings in me that finally disappeared and brought a sense of tranquility and anticipation of some new moment of meaning.

There were seasons in which I thirsted and hungered and touched everything. Summers of leisure and reverie, visions and journeys that terminated much too soon. Summers of contentment that ended with the turning of the leaves and the returning to the fall school life, before an internal readiness, before my internal time could speak and make itself fully known.

And fall seasons too that opened new worlds and enabled slow and gradual meanderings, that brought colors and shapes that awakened radiant energy and rich experiences.

Springs that opened my heart to new discoveries, to the excitement of adventure, to embracings of wind and rain and love. All at once these too were gone, much before I could recognize and cherish the miracles that had awakened in me.

Winters touched my heart and moved me fully into new rhythms of being and relating, into the meaning of chill, into the challenges of danger and adversity, and yet something inside lingered longingly after the signs of spring.

Time has forever followed me, held onto me, experiential time, public time, internal time, external time, duration, continuity, intensity, presence. Past times I want to forget, or remember; a present moment that is stuck or frozen or moves too slowly or too fast; a future that holds so many uncertainties, warnings, forebodings, or one that offers opportunities and entrancements.

It was always time that entered each moment and brought me to my senses, splashed coldly onto the realities, or warmly touched and healed what mattered, time that brought the shadow and the light. Time is in my consciousness now, a constant companion, never letting me just be, without time, but standing by forever and ever.

Time, oh time, you come so suddenly, entering my world, shaking and humbling me, teaching me of mysteries and agonies of living.

Time, slow and gradual, swift and sure, too much of you when not needed, too little in hours of desire.

Time, you linger and endure, you create a sense of now, of yesterday, of tomorrow, forever. You take with you all that is and has been and ever will be.

This one time let it be my time, let it be my timeless choice, let me move things only in accordance with my inner light. Just this once, let this be my timeless time.

I want to hold you back and rush through you, to live again, to feel the joy of silence, to answer the unfinished and the unsettled within me.

Oh time your distant signs are always there; come near me now, let me know the meanings of my fears and courage.

Time, you are my life, my love, my death; ever beginning, ever ending, too soon, too late, too slow, too fast. You enter in every "hello;" in each "goodbye." Time, I surrender to you now. I drift with you into unknown feelings, into unexpressed thoughts, into mysteries of water and earth and air, into sojourns of moon, sun, and stars, into glories with persons near and far, today, tomorrow, yesterday.

REFERENCES

Dreyfus, H. L., & Hall, H. (1982). Husserl's perceptual noema. In *Husserl, intentionality and cognitive science* (pp. 97-123). Cambridge: MIT Press.

Edie, J. M. (1967). Transcendental phenomenology and existentialism. In J. J. Kockelmans (Ed.), *Phenomenology* (pp. 237-251). Garden City, NY: Doubleday.

Follesdal, D. (1982). Husserl's notions of noema. In H. L. Dreyfus (Ed.), *Husserl, intentionality and cognitive science* (pp. 73-90). Cambridge: MIT Press.

Gurwitsch, A. (1966). *Studies in phenomenology and psychology.* Evanston, IL: Northwestern University Press.

Gurwitsch, A. (1967). On the intentionality of consciousness. In J. J. Kockelmans (Ed.), *Phenomenology* (pp. 118-137). Garden City, NY: Doubleday.

Holmes, A. (1975). An explication of Husserl's theory of the noema. *Research in Phenomenology, 5,* 143-153.

Husserl, E. (1931). *Ideas* (W. R. Boyce Gibson, Trans.). London: George Allen & Unwin.

Husserl, E. (1970). *Logical investigations* (J. N. Findlay, Trans.). New York: Humanities Press.

Husserl, E. (1977). *Cartesian meditations: An introduction to metaphysics* (D. Cairns, Trans.). The Hague: Martinus Nijhoff.

Ihde, D. (1977). *Experimental phenomenology.* New York: G. P. Putnam.

Keen, E. (1975). *Doing research phenomenologically.* Unpublished manuscript, Bucknell University, Lewisburg, PA.

Solomon, R. C. (1977). Husserl's concept of noema. In F. Elliston & P. McCormick (Eds.), *Husserl: Expositions and appraisals* (pp. 168-181). Notre Dame, IN: University of Notre Dame Press.

5

EPOCHE,
PHENOMENOLOGICAL REDUCTION,
IMAGINATIVE VARIATION,
AND SYNTHESIS

Evidence from phenomenological research is derived from first-person reports of life experiences.

In accordance with phenomenological principles, scientific investigation is valid when the knowledge sought is arrived at through descriptions that make possible an understanding of the meanings and essences of experience. Husserl (1970b) believed that

> we must exclude all empirical interpretations and existential affirmations, we must take what is inwardly experienced or otherwise inwardly intuited (e.g., in pure fancy) as pure experiences, as our exemplary basis for acts of Ideation. . . . We thus achieve insights in pure phenomenology which is here oriented to *real (reellen)* constituents, whose descriptions are in every way "ideal" and free from . . . presupposition of real existence. (p. 577)

THE EPOCHE PROCESS

Husserl called the freedom from suppositions the *Epoche,* a Greek word meaning to stay away from or abstain. Epoche connects me with my Greek roots and contains the voice of my parents, an expression of their concern, a warning to be alert, to look with care, to see what is really there, and to stay away from everyday habits of knowing things, people, and events.

In the Epoche, we set aside our prejudgments, biases, and preconceived ideas about things. We "invalidate," "inhibit," and "disqualify" all commitments with reference to previous knowledge and experience (Schmitt, 1968, p. 59). The world is placed out of action, while remaining bracketed. However, the world in the bracket has been cleared of ordinary thought and is present before us as a phenomenon to be gazed upon, to be known naively and freshly through a "purified" consciousness.

Husserl (1931, p. 110) contrasted the phenomenological universal Epoche with Cartesian doubt. The phenomenological Epoche does not eliminate everything, does not deny the reality of everything, does not doubt everything—*only the natural attitude,* the biases of everyday knowledge, as a basis for truth and reality. What is doubted are the scientific "facts," the knowing of things in advance, from an external base rather than from internal reflection and meaning. Husserl (1931) asserts that, *"all sciences which relate to this natural world* . . . though they fill me with wondering admiration. . . . *I disconnect them all, I make absolutely no use of their standards, I do not appropriate a single one of the propositions that enter into their systems, even though their evidential value is perfect"* (p. 111).

As I reflect on the nature and meaning of the Epoche, I see it as a preparation for deriving new knowledge but also as an experience in itself, a process of setting aside predilections, prejudices, predispositions, and allowing things, events, and people to enter anew into consciousness, and to look and see them again, as if for the first time. This is not only critical for scientific determination but for living itself—the opportunity for a fresh start, a new beginning, not being hampered by voices of the past that tell us the way things are or voices of the present that direct our thinking. The Epoche is a way of looking and being, an unfettered stance. Whatever or whoever appears in our consciousness is approached with an openness, seeing just what is there and allowing what is there to linger. This is a difficult task and requires that we allow a phenomenon or experience to be just what it is and to come to know it as it presents itself. One's whole life of thinking, valuing, and experiencing flows on, but what captures us in any moment and has validity for us is simply what is there before us as a compelling thing, viewed in an entirely new way. Thus the Epoche gives us an original vantage point, a clearing of mind, space, and time, a holding in abeyance of whatever colors the experience or directs us, anything whatever that has been put into our minds by science or society, or government, or other people, especially one's parents, teachers, and authorities, but also one's friends and enemies. Epoche includes entering a pure internal place, as an open self, ready to embrace life in what it truly offers. From the Epoche, we are challenged to create new ideas, new feelings, new awarenesses and understandings. We are challenged to come to know things with a receptiveness and a presence that lets us be and lets situations and things be, so that we can come to know them just as they appear to us.

The challenge of the Epoche is to be transparent to ourselves, to allow whatever is before us in consciousness to disclose itself so that we may see with new eyes in a naive and completely open manner. Thus, in the process of being transparent in the viewing of things, we also become transparent to ourselves. Although the attentive Ego practices abstention, everything meant is retained but as "mere phenomena," all prior positions are put aside (Husserl, 1977, p. 20). Husserl states that

> what I . . . acquire by it is my pure living, with all the pure subjective processes making this up, and everything meant in them, *purely* as meant in them. . . . The epoche can also be said to be the radical and universal method by which I apprehend myself purely: as Ego with my own pure conscious life, in and by which the entire Objective world exists for me and is precisely as it is for me. (1977, pp. 20-21)

This way of perceiving life calls for looking, noticing, becoming aware, without imposing our prejudgment on what we see, think, imagine, or feel. It is a way of genuine looking that precedes reflectiveness, the making of judgments, or reaching conclusions. We suspend everything that interferes with fresh vision. We simply let what is there stand as it appears, from many angles, perspectives, and signs. Sallis (1982) remarks that the return to beginnings makes the phenomenologist a perpetual beginner. Quoting Husserl, he adds that we "seek to attain the beginnings in a free dedication to the problems themselves and to the demands stemming from them" (p. 115).

In the Epoche, no position whatsoever is taken; every quality has equal value. Only what enters freshly into consciousness, only what appears as appearance, has any validity at all in contacting truth and reality. Nothing is determined in advance. Everything that appears is marked "with a horizon of undetermined determinability" (Husserl, 1977, p. 30) by the possibility of being seen and known in its essential nature and meaning.

Although the process of Epoche requires that everything in the ordinary, everyday sense of knowledge be tabled and put out of action, I, the experiencing person, remain present. I, as a conscious person, am not set aside. On the contrary, with an open, transcendental consciousness, I carry out the Epoche; "I . . . still exist as the doubter and negator of everything" (Husserl, 1970a, p. 77). The self-evidence that I am capable of knowing, in the Epoche, is available to me. I know that I see what I see, feel what I feel, think what I think. What appears before me and in my consciousness is something I know is present regardless of how many others perceive that phenomenon differently. My consciousness is not rooted in them. The Epoche frees me from this bondage to people and things. In the pure Ego state,

> I am the one who performs the epoche, and, even if there are others, and even if they practice the epoche in direct community with me, (they and) all other human beings with their entire act-life are included for me, within my epoche, in the world-phenomenon which, in my epoche, is exclusively mine. The epoche creates a unique sort of philosophical solitude, which is the fundamental methodical requirement for a truly radical philosophy . . . it is I who practice the epoche, I who interrogate, as phenomenon, the world which is now valid for me according to its being and being-such. (Husserl, 1970a, p. 184)

This passage alludes to the difficulty of achieving the Epoche, the pure state of being required for fresh perceiving and experiencing. I must practice the Epoche alone, its nature and intensity require my absolute presence in absolute aloneness. I concentrate fully, and in an enduring way, on what is appearing there before me and in my consciousness. I return to the original nature of my conscious experience. I return to whatever is there in memory, perception, judgment, feeling, whatever is actually there. Everything that appears in my consciousness becomes available for self-referral and self-revelation. The loneliness of such presence, of such consciousness, enables me to target my energy so that I am attending to just what appears and nothing else. The challenge is to silence the directing voices and sounds, internally and externally, to remove from myself manipulating or predisposing influences and to become completely and solely attuned to just what appears, to encounter the phenomenon, as such, with a pure state of mind. There must be individual consciousness first of all, and as the last court of appeal to knowledge. Farber (1943) points out that, "If I as an individual ego 'eliminate' other human beings, I must also suspend all judgments based upon them or involving them . . . with the natural attitude I find myself in the world, along with other human beings. If I abstract from the others, I am alone" (p. 530).

Everything referring to others, their perceptions, preferences, judgments, feelings must be set aside in achieving the Epoche. Only my own perception, my own acts of consciousness, must remain as pointers to knowledge, meaning, and truth. Schmitt (1968) makes this emphatic: "It is I who must decide whether the claims to reality of the objects of experience in particular, and of the world in general, are valid claims. I discover that whatever has sense and validity, has sense and validity for me" (p. 60). Schmitt adds that the world prior to the Epoche and the world following it do not differ in content but only in the way in which I am related to each of them (p. 61). Sartre (1965) catches the sense of this in the following: "The being of an existent is exactly what it appears . . . What it is, it is absolutely, for it reveals itself as it is. The phenomenon can be studied and described as such, for it is absolutely indicative of itself" (p. xlvi).

The process of Epoche, of course, requires unusual, sustained attention, concentration, and presence. However effective we are in attaining the radical change of outlook, what we see requires that it really be there. The thing before us must be delimited in distinction from every other thing (Sallis, 1982, p. 117). It must have a definite identity, a presence that marks it as an entity.

What is before me increasingly comes into meaning as I remain with it, as I linger in its presence, as I open myself to it, as I focus on it in its manifold appearances, in its dimensions, and as a whole. Schleidt (1982) captures the challenge of this kind of presence, involvement and commitment that is the heart of the Epoche process: "A simply prodigious amount of time, spent in presuppositionless observation, is necessary in order to be able . . . to lift the gestalt from its background. . . . Such sustained endeavors can be accomplished only by those whose gaze, through a wholly irrational delight in the beauty of the object, stays riveted to it" (p. 678).

Such an ability to gaze with concentrated and unwavering attention, whether inward or outward, is indeed something that requires patience, a will to enter and stay with whatever it is that interferes until it is removed and an inward clearing is achieved, an opening, an intention directed toward something with clarity and meaning. Every time a distorted thought or feeling enters, the abstention must once again be achieved until there is an open consciousness. I envision a rhythm of being receptive, of being struck with the newness and wonder of just what is before me and what is in me while also being influenced by habit, routine, expectation, and pressure to see things in a certain way until at last, with effort, will, and concentration, I am able to perceive things with an open presence.

In practicing the Epoche, I must focus on some specific situation, person, or issue, find a quiet place in which I can review my current thoughts and feelings regarding this person, situation, or issue. Each time in my review I set aside biases and prejudgments and return with a readiness to look again into my life, to enter with hope and intention of seeing this person, or situation, or issue with new and receptive eyes. This may take several sessions of clearing my mind until I am ready for an authentic encounter.

Another dimension of the Epoche process that encourages an open perception is that of reflective-meditation, letting the preconceptions and prejudgments enter consciousness and leave freely, being just as receptive to them as I am to the unbiased looking and seeing. This meditative procedure is repeated until I experience an internal sense of closure. As I do, I label the prejudgments and write them out. I review the list until its hold on my consciousness is released, until I feel an internal readiness to enter freshly, encounter the situation, issue, or person directly, and receive whatever is offered and come to know it as such.

The Epoche process inclines me toward receptiveness. I am more readily able to meet something or someone and to listen and hear whatever is being presented, without coloring the other's communication with my own habits of thinking, feeling, and seeing, removing the usual ways of labeling or judging, or comparing. I am ready to perceive and know a phenomenon from its appearance and presence.

Although the Epoche is rarely perfectly achieved, the energy, attention, and work involved in reflection and self-dialogue, the intention that underlies the process, and the attitude and frame of reference, significantly reduce the influence of preconceived thoughts, judgments, and biases. Further, regular practice of the Epoche process increases one's competency in achieving a presuppositionless state and in being open to receive whatever appears in consciousness, as such. Despite practice, some entities are simply not "bracketable." There are life experiences that are so severe, intense, and telling, some things that are so ingrained, and some people so attached to or against each other and themselves that clear openness or pure consciousness is virtually an impossibility. On the other hand I believe that with intensive work, prejudices and unhealthy attachments that create false notions of truth and reality can be bracketed and put out of action. The Epoche offers a resource, a process for potential renewal. Approached with dedication and determination, the process can make a difference in what and how we see, hear, and/or view things. Practiced wisely, realistically, and with determination to let go of our prejudices, I believe that the actual nature and essence of things will be disclosed more fully, will reveal themselves to us and enable us to find a clearing and light to knowledge and truth.

PHENOMENOLOGICAL REDUCTION

The Epoche is the first step in coming to know things, in being inclined toward seeing things as they appear, in returning to things themselves, free of prejudgments and preconceptions. In Phenomenological Reduction, the task is that of describing in textural language just what one sees, not only in terms of the external object but also the internal act of consciousness, the experience as such, the rhythm and relationship between phenomenon and self. The qualities of the experience become the focus; the filling in or completion of the nature and meaning of the experience becomes the challenge. The task requires that I look and describe; look again and describe; look again and describe; always with reference to textural qualities—rough and smooth; small and large; quiet and noisy; colorful and bland; hot and cold; stationary and moving; high and low; squeezed in and expansive; fearful and courageous; angry and calm—descriptions that present varying intensities; ranges of shapes, sizes, and spacial qualities; time references; and colors all within an experiential context. So, "to the things themselves," an open field, where everything and anything is available as given in experience. Each angle of perception adds something to one's knowing of the horizons of a phenomenon. The process involves a prereflective description of things just as they appear and a reduction to what is horizonal and thematic. Such an approach to elucidating one's knowledge is known as "Transcendental Phenomenological Reduction." As stated earlier, it is called "Transcendental" because it uncovers the ego for which everything has meaning; "Phenomenological" because the world is transformed into mere phenomena; and "Reduction" in that it leads us back to our own experience of the way things are (Schmitt, 1968, p. 30). Schmitt adds that:

> The world is examined in relation to myself when I try to distinguish those aspects of experience which are genuinely evident from those which I merely assume or suppose to be the case. The subject is examined in relation to the world when I inquire into the beliefs, feelings, and desires which shape the experience. (p. 67)

When we perceive straightforwardly, we focus on the object itself and not the perceiving experience (Miller, 1984, p. 177). We are not so engrossed in our conscious experience that we lose touch with what is actually before us, with the thing itself. It is a matter of shifting attention and focus, but one thing is certain: Our consciousness is directing us meaningfully toward something that continues to remain present however much we may turn inward to our internal experience. Our gaze significantly is on the thing itself, its presence and elucidation. Schutz (1967) puts the matter thus: "Through the attending directed glance of attention and comprehension, the lived experience acquires a mode of being. It *comes to be 'differentiated,' 'thrown into relief,'* and this act of differentiation is nothing other than being comprehended, being the object of the directed glance of attention" (p. 50).

The method of Phenomenological Reduction takes on the character of graded prereflection, reflection, and reduction, with concentrated work aimed at explicating the essential nature of the phenomenon (Husserl, 1931, p. 114). The explication may include perceiving, thinking, remembering, imagining, judging, each of which contains a definite content. Husserl (1931) comments that "every experience in the stream which our reflection can lay hold on has *its own essence open to intuition,* a 'content' which can be considered in its *singularity in and for itself'* (p. 116). The task is to describe its general features, excluding everything that is not immediately within our conscious experience. Phenomenological Reduction is not only a way of seeing but a way of listening with a conscious and deliberate intention of opening ourselves to phenomena as phenomena, in their own right, with their own textures and meanings. Brand (1967), quoting Husserl, further elucidates the process of Phenomenological Reduction:

> I begin, therefore, by questioning that which has in me, under the heading "world," the character of the conscious, the experienced, and the intended, and which is accepted by me as being; I ask what it looks like in its being accepted thus; I ask how I become conscious of it, how I may describe it, how I can designate it, in terms valid for every occasion; how what is subjective in this way manifests itself in different modes, what it looks like in itself, as experienced or as intended as this or that, or what this experiencing itself as experience of the mundane looks like, how it is to be described. . . . That is the general theme opened up by the reduction. (p. 209)

The experiencing person turns inward in reflection, following "the most original information being obtained from myself because here alone is perception the medium" (Husserl, 1931, p. 14). Whatever shines forth in consciousness as I perceive it, reflect on it, imagine it, concentrate on it, is what I attend to—that is what stands out as meaningful for me. Each looking opens new awarenesses that connect with one another, new perspectives that relate to each other, new folds of the manifold features that exist in every phenomenon and that we explicate as we look again and again and again—keeping our eyes turned to the center of the experience and studying what is just before us, exactly as it appears.

Husserl (1931) states that, "We are aware of things not only in perception, but also consciously in recollections, in representations similar to recollections, and also in the free play of fancy . . . they float past us in different 'characterizations' as real, possible, fancied" (p. 117-118). Stay with the phenomenon, let it be in its appearance, view it from different angles, persist to the point of exhausting what it offers during a particular time and place of perceiving and experiencing, or as Husserl advises, "Let us reduce till we reach the stream of pure consciousness" (1931, p. 172). We never totally exhaust the perceptual possibilities of our experience. When the experiencing person is satisfied that the evidence is "complete" the object is said to be given to us *adequately;* we have adequate evidence regarding its existence (Miller, 1984, p. 184).

Although there is always an overlap between looking from one perspective and viewing something as a whole, it is possible to separate the object as a point of focus from my experience of it as a whole, to take one angle of it and look freshly once more, and then another angle, connecting each looking with my conscious experience. I continue this process to the point of unifying the parts into a whole. The process itself is like a visual ray that changes with every experience of perceiving or thinking, shooting forth fresh perceptions with each new moment of seeing as it appears and disappears (Husserl, 1931, p. 172). In *Logical Investigations,* Husserl points out that "we must rather practice 'reflection,' i.e., make these acts themselves, and their immanent meaning-content, our objects. . . . We must deal with them in new acts of intuition and thinking" (1970b, p. 255). Their contents can be contemplated and explicated. The sole aim of the research participant is to see, to describe fully what is seen, just as it is, in such and such a manner (Husserl, 1970a, p. 35).

When the looking and noticing and looking again is complete a more definitely *reflective* process occurs, aimed at grasping the full nature of a phenomenon. To some extent each reflection modifies conscious experience and offers a different perspective of the object. Husserl (1931) emphasizes that, "Only through acts of *experiencing* as reflected on do we know anything of the stream of experience and of its necessary relationship to the pure Ego" (p. 222). The whole process of reducing toward what is texturally meaningful and essential in its phenomenal and experiential components depends on competent and clear reflectiveness, on an ability to attend, recognize, and describe with clarity. Reflection becomes more exact and fuller with continuing attention and perception, with continued looking, with the adding of new perspectives. Reflection becomes more exact through corrections that more completely and accurately present what appears before us. Things become clearer as they are considered again and again. Illusion is undone through correction, through approaching something from a different vantage point, or with a different sense or meaning. Some new dimension becomes thematic and thus alters the perception of what has previously appeared. Husserl relates this to a shift in expectation-horizon (1970a, p. 162). Something else in the phenomenon becomes horizonal; a different kind of expectation; something not seen is now recognized; the expectation of it makes the appearance more likely. In addition, things far away are viewed differently when they come near; inevitably we make corrections as things come into sharper focus and clarity. Husserl (1970a), in commenting on correction, states that

It is easy to see that the change of apperceptive sense takes place through a change of the expectation-horizon of the multiplicities anticipated as normal (i.e., as running on harmoniously). For example, one saw a man, but then, upon touching him, had to reinterpret him as a mannequin (exhibiting itself visually as a man). (p. 162)

Many of us have had the experience of being visually attracted to a bouquet of flowers, moved by their brilliant life colors, their soft petals, grand fragrance, and even their earthy qualities, only to discover on closer look and touch that they are made of silk material. At such a time, our experience radically changes. There have been moments when in utter disbelief I smelled and touched such flowers before being convinced that they were artificial, thus necessitating a correction in my perception and judgment and ultimately arriving at a completely different experience.

In correcting our conscious experience of things we are often influenced by what other people say they see; we are encouraged to look again, from the perspective of another self. Ultimately, we may be seeking an intersubjective description of what appears as phenomenal. We grasp the other's experience with the same perceptual intention that we grasp a thing or event presented to us (Schutz, 1967, p. 106). This self-reference, the return to self, is an essential requirement. We begin with our own perception of the way things are; we see what is before us, first and foremost, with our own eyes, and describe what we see through our own experience of something and the meanings it generates in our awarenesses. Individual perceptions, memories, judgments, reflections, are core and figural in our developing understanding of things and people. Husserl (1970a) comments that we naturally carry out the Epoche and the Reduction from our own vantage point, for ourselves, from our own original self-evidence and consciousness of life-world (p. 253). Following our own self-evidence of what appears to us, we check with others regarding what they perceive, feel, and think. In the process of this kind of careful checking we may revisit the phenomenon and discover something new that alters our knowledge of the thing. Husserl calls this process of interaction with others, and shift in perception and conscious experience, a form of communalization. He states that *"in living with one another* each one can take part in the life of the others. . . . In this communalization there constantly occurs an alteration of validity through reciprocal correction" (1970a, p. 163). My corrections move me toward more accurate and more complete layers of meaning. Kockelmans (1967) observes that, "We penetrate deeper into things and learn to see the more profound 'layers' behind what we first thought to see" (p. 30).

Another dimension of Phenomenological Reduction is the process of horizonalization. Horizons are unlimited. We can never exhaust completely our experience of things no matter how many times we reconsider them or view them. A new horizon arises each time that one recedes. It is a never-ending process and, though we may reach a stopping point and discontinue our perception of something, the possibility for discovery is unlimited. The horizonal makes of conscious experience a continuing mystery, one that opens regions of laughter and hope or pain and anguish as these enter our conscious life. We may think that some perception of experience will forever remain, but the contents of conscious life appear and disappear. No horizon lasts indefinitely, regardless of wish, hope, or fear.

In Phenomenological Reduction we return to the self; we experience things that exist in the world from the vantage point of self-awareness, self-reflection, and self-knowledge. Things enter conscious awareness and recede only to return again. Something essential is recovered: "The phenomenological reductions make it possible for the mind to discover its own nature; originally lost in the world, the mind can find itself again by means of these reductions" (Kockelmans, 1967, p. 222).

Each horizon as it comes into our conscious experience is the grounding or condition of the phenomenon that gives it a distinctive character. We consider each of the horizons and the textural qualities that enable us to understand an experience. When we horizonalize, each phenomenon has equal value as we seek to disclose its nature and essence. Keen (1975), for example, in exploring the horizons of a student's question felt uncomfortable "because I had the vague sense that he was begging for something" (p. 28). The "begging" sense was Keen's immediate, prereflective experience of his student. As he reflected on the begging phenomenon, he decided to avoid the student as he would "beggars on the street" (1975, p. 29). Keen exclaims:

I felt uncomfortable about his question [of whether he should become a psychologist] because I had the vague sense that he was begging me for something. That was an immediate and prereflective experience of him at that moment, and it is important to allow that experience to be what it was, to recall it and to articulate its content. Having done so, we need now to reflect on that experience. (1975, p. 28)

Keen continues, "It was horizonal to my experience of him as begging me for something. It is only by careful examining of my experience that these horizons became apparent" (1975, p. 29). On further reflection, Keen discovered that the student reminded him of his patients and also with youthful ambivalence toward elders, the student's relationship to his father, and a member of the dispossessed class coping with the privileged class, and finally that perhaps his student was asking for something he never got from his father—acceptance and respect (p. 31). These horizons were constituents of the phenomenon of "begging" in a relationship and provided a way of describing the bracketed phenomenon, "begging."

The final challenge of Phenomenological Reduction is the construction of a complete textural description of the experience. Such a description, beginning with the Epoche and going through a process of returning to the thing itself, in a state of openness and freedom, facilitates clear seeing, makes possible identity, and encourages the looking again and again that leads to deeper layers of meaning. Throughout, there is an interweaving of person, conscious experience, and phenomenon. In the process of explicating the phenomenon, qualities are recognized and described; every perception is granted equal value, nonrepetitive constituents of the experience are linked thematically, and a full description is derived. The prereflective and reflective components of Phenomenological Reduction enable an uncovering of the nature and meaning of experience, bringing the experiencing person to a self-knowledge and a knowledge of the phenomenon. Or stated differently:

Each experience is considered in its singularity, and for itself. Within the brackets, the phenomenon is perceived and described in its totality, in a fresh and open way, a graded series of reductions coming from a transcendental state, a total differentiated description of the most essential constituents of the phenomenon. (Moustakas, 1986, p. 16)

To summarize, the steps of Phenomenological Reduction include: *Bracketing,* in which the focus of the research is placed in brackets, everything else is set aside so that the entire research process is rooted solely on the topic and question; *horizonalizing,* every statement initially is treated as having equal value. Later, statements irrelevant to the topic and question as well as those that are repetitive or overlapping are deleted, leaving only the *Horizons* (the textural meanings and invariant constituents of the phenomenon); *Clustering the Horizons Into Themes*; and *Organizing the Horizons and Themes Into a Coherent Textural Description* of the phenomenon.

A description of the essential constituents of pure depression is excerpted from Keen's study (1984), "Emerging From Depression."

Depression is experienced as the stoppage of time, the emptiness of space, and the reification of others. Time stops; development of myself, of situations, and of relationships all grind to a halt. Everything appears static, dead, with no change except a progressive deterioration like rusting or rotting. Most of all, the future ceases being really future, really new, unknown, fruitful. Rather, the future seems to promise only a dreary repetition of the past. Space is empty. There are things, but they have lost their importance. My house, once a haven and a home, is a mere building, drained of its echoes of vitality and love. My clothes, once full of interest for me, now hang gaping stupidly in my closet. My books are dead, my tennis racquet a mere thing. And other people—their development in time, like my own, gave the future its hope and cast meaning into spaces and places—now are mere things, walking and talking like manikins, mechanically echoing scripts written long ago. (p. 804)

IMAGINATIVE VARIATION

Following Phenomenological Reduction, the next step in the research process is that of Imaginative Variation. The task of Imaginative Variation is to seek possible meanings through the utilization of imagination, varying the frames of reference, employing polarities and reversals, and approaching the phenomenon from divergent perspectives, different positions, roles, or functions. The aim is to arrive at structural descriptions of an experience, the underlying and precipitating factors that account for what is being experienced; in other words the "how" that speaks to conditions that illuminate the "what" of experience. How did the experience of the phenomenon come to be what it is?

Describing the essential structures of a phenomenon is the major task of Imaginative Variation. In this there is a free play of fancy; any perspective is a possibility and is permitted to enter into consciousness. Husserl (1931) points to how the process evolves:

> The Eidos, the *pure essence,* can be exemplified intuitively in the data of experience, data of perception, memory, and so forth, but just as readily . . . in the play of fancy we bring spatial shapes of one sort or another to birth, melodies, social happenings, and so forth, or live through fictitious acts of everyday life. (p. 57)

Variation is targeted toward meanings and depends on intuition as a way of integrating structures into essences. In *Cartesian Meditations* (1977), Husserl states that, "Every imaginable sense, every imaginable being, whether the latter is called immanent or transcendent, falls within the domain of transcendental subjectivity, as the subjectivity that constitutes sense and being" (p. 84). We find in fantasy the potential meaning of something that makes the invisible visible (1931, p. 40). The uncovering of the essences, the focusing on pure possibilities, is central in the Imaginative Variation process. In this phase of the process the structures of the experience are revealed; these are the conditions that must exist for something to appear. Kockelmans (1967) comments that, "Reduction leads us from the realm of facts to that of general essences . . . [it] is the methodic procedure through which we raise our knowledge from the level of facts to the sphere of 'ideas' " (p. 30). For example, in considering the red of individual objects we know that there is a generic *redness* as such. No matter how many variations we perceive in the color red, all have the redness of red running through them. We can arrive at this intuition only through an imaginative integration of what is common in all the shadings of red.

In Imaginative Variation the world disappears, existence no longer is central, anything whatever becomes possible. The thrust is away from facts and measurable entities and toward meanings and essences; in this instant, intuition is not empirical but purely imaginative in character. Husserl (1931) emphasizes that, *"pure essential truths do not make the slightest assertion concerning* facts; hence from them *alone* we are not able to infer even the pettiest truth concerning the fact-world" (p. 57). The Imaginative Variation process includes a reflective phase in which many possibilities are examined and explicated reflectively. Free imaginative fancy is coupled with reflective explication giving body, detail, and descriptive fullness to the search for essences. Casey (1977) has stated that in Imaginative Variation we contemplate as many imagined objects or events as possible; existent or not; an imaginary unicorn, for example, is a purely possible entity (p. 75).

Imaginative Variation enables the researcher to derive structural themes from the textural descriptions that have been obtained through Phenomenological Reduction. We imagine possible structures of time, space, materiality, causality, and relationship to self and to others. These are universal structural groundings connected with textural figures. Through Imaginative Variation the researcher understands that there is not a single inroad to truth, but that countless possibilities emerge that are intimately connected with the essences and meanings of an experience.

The steps of Imaginative Variation include:

1. Systematic varying of the possible structural meanings that underlie the textural meanings;
2. Recognizing the underlying themes or contexts that account for the emergence of the phenomenon;
3. Considering the universal structures that precipitate feelings and thoughts with reference to the phenomenon, such as the structure of time, space, bodily concerns, materiality, causality, relation to self, or relation to others;
4. Searching for exemplifications that vividly illustrate the invariant structural themes and facilitate the development of a structural description of the phenomenon.

Borrowing again from Keen's study (1984), the structural emphases are included in this excerpt:

Emerging from depression involves not the disappearance of a symptom but the reappearance, reinvention, or rediscovery of a self with a past and a future. My present life, which leads from the past into the future, matters when it is part of a historical unfolding within which I can place myself in an integral part. Having a job, being a parent, engaging in crafts, for example, *can* supply such a story. In depression, these ordinary aspects of life have been neutralized—rendered meaningless—by the death themes of depression: the stoppage of time, the emptiness of space, and the reification of people. The reestablishment of a future, the refurnishing of space with significance and vitality, and the repersonification of others are all implicated in reinventing myself and emerging from depression. (p. 808)

SYNTHESIS OF MEANINGS AND ESSENCES

The final step in the phenomenological research process is the intuitive integration of the fundamental textural and structural descriptions into a unified statement of the essences of the experience of the phenomenon as a whole. This is the guiding direction of the eidetic sciences, the establishment of a knowledge of essences (Husserl, 1931, p. 44).

Essence, as Husserl (1931) employs this concept, means that which is common or universal, the condition or quality without which a thing would not be what it is (p. 43). Sartre (1965) refers to essence as the principle of the series, the "concatenation of appearances" (p. xlvi). He states that, "The essence finally is radically severed from the individual appearance which manifests it, since on principle it is that which must be able to be manifested by an infinite series of individual manifestations" (p. xlviii).

The essences of any experience are never totally exhausted. The fundamental textural-structural synthesis represents the essences at a particular time and place from the vantage point of an individual researcher following an exhaustive imaginative and reflective study of the phenomenon. Husserl (1931) concludes that "every physical property draws us on into infinities of experience; and that every multiplicity of experience, however lengthily drawn out, still leaves the way open to closer and novel thing-determinations; and so on, *in infinitum*" (pp. 54-55).

Keen (1984) presents a synthesis of the meanings and essences of the experience of emerging from depression in the following:

The final truth seems to be that emerging from depression is never really complete. The work of remembering, and feeling the sadness, must be renewed a little every day. The fight into distractions avoids that sadness and makes us more cheerful, perhaps. But it is the superficial good cheer of the game show host, or the empty pride of the dedicated professional achiever. Addiction to happiness is no less an addiction than the vilest narcotic. Withdrawal provokes panic. Flexibility is gone; dependency is complete.

The sadness of memories is far preferable to the happiness of subclinical depression, for it throws into relief the really good things in life, and makes them shine forth. In this way, ecstasy and tragedy are two sides of the same coin. Depression can be devastating, but having emerged, I find that depression is enriching and enlivening as I live the reinvented self, born in the struggle of emergence. (p. 810)

CONCLUDING COMMENTS

Understanding the nature, meanings, and essences of Epoche, Phenomenological Reduction, Imaginative Variation, and Synthesis is necessary in order to conduct phenomenological research. Through phenomenology a significant methodology is developed for investigating human experience and for deriving knowledge from a state of pure consciousness. One learns to see naively and freshly again, to value conscious experience, to respect the evidence of one's senses, and to move toward an intersubjective knowing of things, people, and everyday experiences.

REFERENCES

Brand, G. (1967). Intentionality, reduction and intentional analysis in Husserl's later manuscripts. In J. J. Kockelmans (Ed.), *Phenomenology* (pp. 197-217). Garden City, NY: Doubleday.

Casey, E. S. (1977). Imagination and phenomenological method. In F. Elliston & P. McCormick (Eds.), *Husserl: Expositions and appraisals* (pp. 70-82). Notre Dame, IN: University of Notre Dame.

Farber, M. (1943). *The foundation of phenomenology.* Albany: SUNY Press.

Husserl. E. (1931). *Ideas* (W. R. Boyce Gibson, Trans.). London: George Allen & Unwin.

Husserl, E. (1970a). *The crisis of European sciences and transcendental phenomenology: An introduction to phenomenological philosophy* (D. Carr, Trans.). Evanston, IL: Northwestern University Press.

Husserl, E. (1970b). *Logical investigations* (J. N. Findlay, Trans.). New York: Humanities Press.

Husserl, E. (1977). *Cartesian meditations: An introduction to metaphysics* (D. Cairns, Trans.). The Hague: Martinus Nijhoff.

Keen, E. (1975). *Doing research phenomenologically*. Unpublished manuscript, Bucknell University, Lewisburg, PA.

Keen, E. (1984). Emerging from depression. *American Behavioral Scientist, 27*(6), 801-812.

Kockelmans, J. J. (Ed.). (1967). What is phenomenology? In *Phenomenology* (pp. 24-36). Garden City, NY: Doubleday.

Miller, I. (1984). The phenomenological reduction. In *Perception and temporal awareness* (pp. 175-198). Cambridge: MIT Press.

Moustakas, C. (1986). *Transcendental phenomenology*. Unpublished manuscript, Center for Humanistic Studies, Detroit, MI.

Sallis, J. (1982). The identities of the things themselves. *Research in Phenomenology, xii*, 113-126.

Sartre, J. P. (1965). Introduction: The pursuit of being. In *Being and nothingness* (pp. xlv-lxvii) (H. E. Barnes, Trans.). New York: Citadel Press.

Schleidt, W. M. (1982). Review of Lorenz' The foundation of ethology. *Contemporary Psychology, 27*(9), 677-678.

Schmitt, R. (1968). Husserl's transcendental-phenomenological reduction. In J. J. Kockelmans (Ed.), *Phenomenology* (pp. 58-68). Garden City, NY: Doubleday.

Schutz, A. (1967). *The phenomenology of the social world* (G. Walsh & F. Lehnert, Trans.). Evanston, IL: Northwestern University Press.

⚅⚅
6
⚅⚅

METHODS AND PROCEDURES
FOR CONDUCTING
HUMAN SCIENCE RESEARCH

In deriving scientific evidence in phenomenological investigations, the researcher establishes and carries out a series of methods and procedures that satisfy the requirements of an organized, disciplined and systematic study. These include:

1. Discovering a topic and question rooted in autobiographical meanings and values, as well as involving social meanings and significance;
2. Conducting a comprehensive review of the professional and research literature;
3. Constructing a set of criteria to locate appropriate co-researchers;
4. Providing co-researchers with instructions on the nature and purpose of the investigation, and developing an agreement that includes obtaining informed consent, insuring confidentiality, and delineating the responsibilities of the primary researcher and research participant, consistent with ethical principles of research;
5. Developing a set of questions or topics to guide the interview process;

6. Conducting and recording a lengthy person-to-person interview that focuses on a bracketed topic and question. A follow-up interview may also be needed;

7. Organizing and analyzing the data to facilitate development of individual textural and structural descriptions, a composite textural description, a composite structural description, and a synthesis of textural and structural meanings and essences.

The above methodological requirements may be organized in terms of Methods of Preparation, Methods of Collecting Data, and Methods of Organizing and Analyzing Data. A method offers a systematic way of accomplishing something orderly and disciplined, with care and rigor. Procedures or techniques make up a method, provide a direction and steps to be followed, and move a study into action. Every method in human science research is open ended. There are no definitive or exclusive requirements. Each research project holds its own integrity and establishes its own methods and procedures to facilitate the flow of the investigation and the collection of data.

In the sections that follow, methods and procedures for conducting human science research are discussed and illustrated.

METHODS OF PREPARATION

Formulating the Question

The first challenge of the researcher, in preparing to conduct a phenomenological investigation, is to arrive at a topic and question that have both social meaning and personal significance. The question must be stated in clear and concrete terms. The key words of the question should be defined, discussed, and clarified so that the intent and purpose of the investigation are evident. The position of each key word, or focus, of the question determines what is primary in pursuing the topic and what data will be collected.

In phenomenological research, the question grows out of an intense interest in a particular problem or topic. The researcher's excitement and curiosity inspire the search. Personal history brings the core of the problem into focus. As the fullness of the topic emerges, strands and tangents of it may complicate an articulation of a manageable and specific question. Yet this process of permitting aspects of the topic to enter into awareness is essential in the formulation of a core question that will remain viable and alive throughout the investigation. A human science research question has definite characteristics:

1. It seeks to reveal more fully the essences and meanings of human experience;
2. It seeks to uncover the qualitative rather than the quantitative factors in behavior and experience;
3. It engages the total self of the research participant, and sustains personal and passionate involvement;
4. It does not seek to predict or to determine causal relationships;
5. It is illuminated through careful, comprehensive descriptions, vivid and accurate renderings of the experience, rather than measurements, ratings, or scores.

Illustrations of the Topic and Question

In applications of phenomenological research presented in this chapter, I have selected examples from the published literature as well as from studies in which I served as a guide or reviewer of the research design and methodology proposed by the primary researcher.

LaCourse's Study of Time: Personal and Social Meanings

To illustrate the personal and social groundings of the topic and question, I have selected what I regard as a good example of a design and methodology for investigating the experience of time.

In considering time as the topic, LaCourse (1990) first explores its autobiographical and social significance. She describes her personal background and its relationship to the topic and question.

The study of time beckons to me, I think, because issues of time are prominent in my own life. I have strong feelings about time. I love life, and since in so many ways time is life, I love my time. I put careful thought into how I will use it, and I jealously guard against excessive intrusions into my time by others. I have always seen time as a precious commodity. . . . And yet so often I feel I am in conflict with time. There is a lack of clarity within me as to the meaning of time in my life and how I can best live in harmony with it. I am puzzled, intrigued, and frustrated by time, and challenged to learn more about it. It is this challenge that leads me to consider studying time. I am excited by the idea of reading about it, thinking about it, listening to others talk about their experiences with it, and eventually coming to a place where my understanding of time has been expanded, my perspective broadened, and quite possibly, as a side benefit, my relationship with it enhanced. (p. 7)

I wonder how this feeling that there is not enough time came about. Have I made my life overly complicated, failing along the way to develop the self-discipline and time-management skills needed to cope? Probably this is true to some extent, but I believe my sense of time pressure is due in greater part to my perception of time as accelerating as I grow older, and my consequent anxiety about the passage of time. (p. 8)

I am drawn to a study of time in part because I have had difficulty living in harmony with time. I have been in conflict as to how to be in relationship with other people, and still be true to my privacy and other time needs. Finding the delicate balance in time usage which is necessary in order to achieve objectives without becoming rigid, overly organized, or over-extended has been a huge challenge for me. (p. 12)

The social meaning and relevance of LaCourse's topic is connected to tendencies in society to seek to control and exploit time for purposes of economic production and security, presumably for purposes of "health, happiness, and effectiveness in living" (p. 3). She points out that often the focus in society is on *past* traumas or *future* events and opportunities rather than on the present. She states that, "an exploration of . . . the continuity of time . . . from the perspective of co-researchers could provide valuable information" on balancing personal and social require-ments (pp. 4-5). Another social concern with reference to time relates to time management issues and the stress individuals experience as a result of poor time management skills.

LaCourse's Study of Time: Formulating the Question

LaCourse formulated her question and defined its key words, as follows:

My research question as it now stands is: "How do people perceive and describe their experience of time?" The major components of this question are "how," "perceive," "describe," "experience," and "time." . . . Use of the word "how" facilitates clear, concise wording of the question and denotes my openness to anything whatever that may emerge about time in the course of my interviews with co-researchers. The word *"perceive"* implies something about the relativity of time. . . . Time is perceived differently by different people, and by the same person in different situations. The cliches, "time flies when you're having fun" or "I lived a lifetime in a moment," speak to this. Also, time drags for most people when waiting or doing something unpleasant. The word *"describe"* refers to *what time is and means* for co-researchers. The word *"experience"* is a way of pointing to the fact that I will be seeking comprehensive stories from the research participants of how they perceive and describe time in their everyday lived experience. (pp. 2-3)

Locating and Selecting the Research Participants

There are no in-advance criteria for locating and selecting the research participants. General considerations include: age, race, religion, ethnic and cultural factors, gender, and political and economic factors. Essential criteria include: the research participant has experienced the phenomenon, is intensely interested in understanding its nature and meanings, is willing to participate in a lengthy interview and (perhaps a follow-up interview), grants the investigator the right to tape-record, possibly videotape the interview, and publish the data in a dissertation and other publications.

Locating and Selecting the Research Participants:
Fraelich's Investigation of Presence

Fraelich (1989) investigated the experience of psychologist-psychotherapist "presence" in relationship to the client. In locating participants and enlisting them for the study, Fraelich prepared a statement describing the nature and purpose of the study and sought to locate psychologists-psychotherapists who regarded "presence" as a necessary component of therapeutic effectiveness. The "statement of instructions" was placed (with permission from the director of training) in the mailboxes of psychologists-psychotherapists working in a large community psychological clinic. Fraelich comments that, "Each person who replied was then contacted by me and a 10 to 20 minute pre-interview meeting was arranged at the clinic at times mutually agreeable to both of us" (p. 66). From the interview and a discussion of the nature and purpose of the study, Fraelich determined whether the volunteer was an appropriate co-researcher for his proposed investigation. This depended on whether the co-researcher was willing to join Fraelich in an open-ended investigation of "presence," willing to commit the necessary time and work that would be involved, willing for the interview to be tape-recorded and the data from it used in a doctoral dissertation and publications.

In his preliminary instructions to co-researchers, Fraelich conveyed to them that he would share with them the specific material from their interview that he would use, that he would remove all identifying data, including the name of the co-researcher, and that the co-researcher would be free to withdraw from the study at any time. When a mutual agreement was reached, a "permission form" was signed. A date and time for the lengthy interview were mutually agreed upon. The co-researcher was asked to immerse him- or herself in incidents that stood out in the experience of psychologist-psychotherapist presence in interviews with clients, and to bring to awareness whatever awakened in descriptive meanings of presence. Fraelich comments, "I hoped that by doing this, each participant would be able to bring a rich set of experiences into the interview" (p. 68). He adds,

> Each participant was informed not only of the true nature of the study but was encouraged to become a research participant on equal footing with me. An active attempt was made to recognize the participant as a co-researcher. Each participant was encouraged to join with me as a truthful seeker of knowledge and understanding with regard to the phenomenon of presence. (p. 68) [Reprinted by permission of the author]

Following the pre-interview meeting, Fraelich

> reflected upon my research question and re-envisioned the phenomenon that I wanted to come to understand. From this perspective, an opening statement, to be read to the participant just prior to the beginning of the interview, was prepared. The purpose of the statement was to provide a standard way to begin the interview and to present an opening remark geared to encourage the participant to initiate his or her own search and to again convey the overall purpose and intent of the interview. (p. 68) [Reprinted by permission of the author]

To illustrate final procedures that are employed in selecting co-researchers, I have placed in Appendix A, from Trumbull's (1993) study of coronary artery bypass surgery, his "Letter to Co-Researchers" and his "Participant Release Agreement." They present necessary details of the agreement and inform the co-researcher of the nature and purpose of the study.

Trumbull also provided a summary guide. I present an abbreviated, edited version of it, to illustrate it as a model of helpful instructions to potential co-researchers.

Summary Guide of Study for Potential Co-Researchers

As a research project required for the PhD degree in clinical psychology, I will complete a dissertation on the topic "What is the experience of undergoing coronary artery bypass surgery?" The topic was chosen after my uncle and father had this surgical procedure. I will conduct a literature review to learn about prior published works on this topic. Since I am interested in descriptions and meanings connected with your experience, I will use qualitative research methods in obtaining the essences of your experience. I will interview 12 to 15 co-researchers and adhere to the ethical principles of human science research. The structural and textural descriptions that I will be seeking will be formulated into a synthesis of the experience as a whole.

On completion of the study, Trumbull sent to each co-researcher a letter expressing his appreciation for their contribution to the knowledge of the nature, quality, meaning, and essence of the experience of undergoing coronary artery bypass surgery. An abbreviated version of the letter appears in Appendix B.

Trumbull also sent his complete analysis of all of the data to each of his co-researchers and requested a response as to its accuracy and any changes that would present more clearly or fully the experience of undergoing coronary artery bypass surgery.

ETHICAL PRINCIPLES

Human science researchers are guided by the ethical principles on research with human participants. The studies referred to in this volume maintained the necessary ethical standards, established clear agreements with the research participants, recognized the necessity of confidentiality and informed consent, and developed procedures for insuring full disclose of the nature, purpose, and requirements of the research project. All of the studies were qualitative, involved participants who volunteered to be co-researchers, emphasized processes that were open-ended and methods and procedures that could be shifted, and permitted alternatives in response to participants' ideas and suggestions, as needed for accuracy, safety, and comfort. Co-researchers were free to withdraw at any time. The investigators also provided detailed information regarding the nature and purpose of the study in response to co-researchers' questions prior to selecting research participants; also during the study and following the analysis of data. Because minimal risk was involved in terms of the health and well-being of the participant, rarely did the need for terminating an interview arise, or the need for immediate therapeutic support, or for referral for psychotherapeutic help. In all studies, the designs and processes of data collection were completely open for discussion. The co-researchers often contributed effective ways of guiding the long interview. Information that the investigator considered private, and possibly damaging, was removed or disguised to protect the identity of the research participant. Confidentiality was maintained relevant to the data to be used unless the co-researcher was fully informed and agreed to its use.

The kind of debriefing, suggested by Blanck, Bellack, Rosnow, Rotheram-Borus, and Schooler (1992) for the removal of "any misconceptions and anxieties that the participants have about the research and to leave them with a sense of dignity" (p. 961), was not required in the qualitative studies reported here. Because the interviews were conversational and open-ended, misconceptions were clarified as they occurred, open disclosures were accepted and supported. The importance of self-reports in data collection was emphasized so that the research participant felt his or her contributions were valued as new knowledge on the topic and as an illumination of meanings inherent in the question. The research participant could also review and confirm or alter the research data to correspond to her or his perception of the experience.

VALIDATION OF DATA

A good example of validation of data is borrowed from Humphrey's (1991) study of "searching for life's meaning."

Humphrey interviewed 14 co-researchers in exploring his topic and question. He sent them copies of his synthesis of the textural-structural description of their experience. He requested of each participant that she or he carefully examine the unified description of the search for life's meaning and that additions and corrections be made. Of the 13 who responded, 8 stated that the synthesis was accurate and that no changes were needed. Humphrey comments:

> The fourteenth was contacted twice by mail and twice by phone, but did not respond.
> Three offered important suggestions concerning omissions or questions of emphasis. Two indicated that they did not believe that the "dark side" of their search for meaning—the terrifying sense of meaningless or universal chaos which they sometimes experienced—was adequately represented. . . . This was an eye-opening confrontation to me, inviting me to look more closely at my own fear of the existential void and hidden desperation which might lead one to hold onto something rather than risking the apparent abyss of meaninglessness. I had thought that my heuristic exploration of my own search had been thorough. . . . I had been aware that two transcribers had resigned from continuing to work on my project while they were working on two different research interviews right at the point at which the participants were describing comprehensively their fear of meaninglessness. Clearly this is a powerful and difficult aspect of the search for meaning which some of us would rather avoid. Fortunately, the step of participant validation highlighted the reduced emphasis on this aspect. I returned to . . . my own search and also reexamined the research interviews. (pp. 81-82) [Reprinted by permission of the author]

Humphrey revised the "synthesis" statement, significantly expanding the qualities and meanings of the dark side of searching for life's meaning.

REVIEW OF THE PROFESSIONAL
AND RESEARCH LITERATURE

Another method of preparing to conduct a phenomenological study involves review of the professional and research literature connected with the research topic and question. The investigator assesses the prior relevant studies; distinguishes their designs, methodologies, and findings from the investigator's own study; and indicates what new knowledge he or she is seeking and expects to obtain.

Cooper (1989) has identified four major kinds of literature review. The *integrative* review presents the "state of knowledge" relevant to a topic and draws conclusions from the many separate studies that are reviewed. These studies typically define the problem, outline the methods of data collection, evaluate the data, make analyses and interpretations, and present the findings. The *theoretical* review analyzes the theories that account for the existence of the phenomenon. The *methodological* review examines the research methods developed and utilized in the published works. The *thematic* review organizes the core themes presented in the studies and presents their findings within the core themes. Regardless of the approach, both formal and informal methods are used.

In conducting a review, Cooper (1989) emphasizes employing multiple channels. These might include a computer search for abstracts of the psychological and educational literature (e.g., PsychINFO and ERIC), a computer search of the *Social Science Citation Index, Books in Print,* and *Dissertation Abstracts International* from which relevant abstracts are obtained and become important resources for more extensive study.

Manual and informal sources might include a follow-up of references cited in review papers on the topic as well as those appearing on book lists obtained from library indexes; browsing in bookstores and libraries; contacts with experts on the topic; conversations with professors and other students; documents of relevant government agencies; studies of comments on the topic from past reviews of the literature; and attendance at professional meetings. In determining the key descriptors for locating references, the *Thesaurus of Psychological Index Terms* and comprehensive dictionaries are utilized.

From his survey of 57 authors of research reviews covering psychology and education, Cooper (1989) determined that the significance of the references were derived from various searches. The *most central* were: computer searches of abstract databases, such as ERIC and Psych-INFO; manual searches of abstract databases; computer searches of a citation index, such as SSCI; manual searches of a citation index; references in review papers written by others; and references in books written by others (p. 59). The most frequently used were: references in review papers written by others, references in books written by others, communication with people who typically share information with the researcher, references in nonreview papers from journals, and computer searches of abstract databases (Cooper, 1989, p. 59).

Cooper (1989) summarizes the purposes for using the technical and nontechnical literature. The technical literature includes: *theoretical sensitivity* regarding concepts and relationships in order to look for evidence from one's own research that confirms or rejects the relevancy of the concepts and relationships and in order to learn ways of approaching and interpreting one's data; *secondary sources of data* may provide useful interviews and field notes as well as descriptive materials of relevant events, actions, and perspectives of the research participant; *guides to questions* to explore with one's co-researchers; *ideas helpful in developing one's theory*; and *supplementary validation* of the accuracy of one's research findings (pp. 51-52).

The nontechnical literature "can be used as primary data, especially historical and biographical studies. In most studies they [i.e., letters, biographies, diaries, reports, videotapes, and newspapers] are important sources of data, supplementing the most usual interviews and observations" (Cooper, 1989, p. 55).

Trumbull's Study of Coronary Artery Bypass Surgery: Literature Review

Trumbull (1993) in his phenomenological study of coronary artery bypass surgery conducted a computer search of the Medline database covering the years 1980-1991. He located 6,919 citations of articles and dissertations. Eliminating the nonhuman and foreign language studies and restricting the list to psychological, psychiatric, psychosomatic, and psychosocial investigations, he reduced the list to 82 titles.

In a second database, using PsychINFO and covering the same 1980-1991 years, Trumbull obtained a printout of 30 citations, 5 of which were dissertations. Of these, 27 involved psychological and psychosocial impact and the quality-of-life effects of bypass surgery; 2 dealt with the impact on spouse and family; and 1 focused on medication and its impact, after bypass surgery.

Trumbull also used *Sociological Abstracts* for the same period. No citations appeared in the printout relevant to psychological and psychosocial aspects of bypass surgery. However, repeating the search and adding "heart disease," 27 citations appeared; 26 of these were irrelevant to his question. The one relevant listing was with reference to psychosocial impact, outcomes, and quality-of-life effects as a result of bypass surgery.

The fourth database used was *Magazine Index,* which included popular magazine citations. From this, three citations were relevant—two autobiographical accounts of persons who had the surgery and one on psychosocial impact, outcomes, and quality of life.

In his "hands on" search in a major library system, Trumbull found nine books in print that were relevant to his study of the experience of undergoing coronary artery bypass surgery. The list included four that presented educational and informational materials on diet and lifestyle changes aimed at preventing further problems following the surgery; three were autobiographical accounts of individuals who had the surgery; and two were on prevention of further problems through diet and lifestyle changes following surgery.

Trumbull located only one qualitative study. In this study a content analysis of bypass surgery was undertaken.

The research generally, in articles, dissertations, and books, focused on isolated aspects of behavior associated with quantitative outcomes and effects of the coronary artery bypass surgery.

METHODS OF DATA COLLECTION

Typically in the phenomenological investigation the long interview is the method through which data is collected on the topic and question.

The phenomenological interview involves an informal, interactive process and utilizes open-ended comments and questions. Although the primary researcher may in advance develop a series of questions aimed at evoking a comprehensive account of the person's experience of the phenomenon, these are varied, altered, or not used at all when the co-researcher shares the full story of his or her experience of the bracketed question.

Often the phenomenological interview begins with a social conversation or a brief meditative activity aimed at creating a relaxed and trusting atmosphere. Following this opening, the investigator suggests that the co-researcher take a few moments to focus on the experience, moments of particular awareness and impact, and then to describe the experience fully. The interviewer is responsible for creating a climate in which the research participant will feel comfortable and will respond honestly and comprehensively.

Stevick: Study of Anger

In her study of anger, Stevick (1971) chose her research participants on the basis of their ability "to provide full descriptions of their lived experience of anger" (p. 135). Because her research participants were former students and friends (within the age range of her design—between 15 and 18), Stevick knew which girls would be able to provide comprehensive descriptions of their experience of anger. She states, "Method and phenomenon must dialogue; what method will best allow the full emergence of the phenomenon in all its aspects: the situation, the behavior and experience of the subject?" (p. 135). Stevick opened each interview with a broad statement: "Try to remember the last time you were angry and tell me anything you can about the situation, about what you felt, did or said." Additional questions were asked spontaneously during the interview "for clarification and fuller descriptions of their replies" (p. 135). The following excerpt from Stevick's investigation illustrates the open-ended interview process in phenomenological research.

E: Try to remember one of the last times you were angry and tell me about the situation, how you felt and acted, and what you said.

S: The last time I was mad it was at my grandmother. I wished she was dead; she's really always getting behind you no matter what you do. It's always wrong, no matter what you do. Like last night we came home, she wanted us to wash clothes. We said, no, that we were working today, so we'd do it later. So she gets all mad and tells us, "Oh, you never do anything right; you never do anything around here." So anything you do is always wrong. So being angry means you can't stand a person . . .

E: Do you do or say anything when she starts doing that?

S: I never say anything when she does it, cause I know to keep my mouth shut; she just likes to hear herself talk. So I just say to myself, "Let her talk and she'll have to shut up sooner or later."

E: While you're angry you said that you think of how you hate her, then later you tell yourself you're going to get away. Do you cool off by telling yourself that?

S: Yes, I say, "Well, sooner or later you'll be away from here, so . . .

E: Do you say or do anything when you get angry at other people?

S: I cry sometimes. When they really say something to you, you just go up to your room and just say, "Why does it have to be me living in this house with these people." And you just cry over it and it's better after you finish crying.

E: Do you ever talk back?

S: Sometimes, usually she doesn't hear me cause if she heard me it would all be over . . .

E: What is this feeling like, that you have to let something out?

S: Because if you don't, well, I feel like it has to come out; I either talk to somebody or I cry or say to myself, "You're going to get out of here." Because if you don't it's all going to build up. (Stevick, 1971, pp. 137-138)

GENERAL INTERVIEW GUIDE

Sometimes a general interview guide, or topical guide, is used when the co-researcher's story has not tapped into the experience qualitatively and with sufficient meaning and depth. Broad questions, such as the following, may also facilitate the obtaining of rich, vital, substantive descriptions of the co-researcher's experience of the phenomenon. The language and timely way in which the questions are posed facilitates full disclosures of the co-researcher's experience.

1. What dimensions, incidents and people intimately connected with the experience stand out for you?
2. How did the experience affect you? What changes do you associate with the experience?
3. How did the experience affect significant others in your life?
4. What feelings were generated by the experience?
5. What thoughts stood out for you?
6. What bodily changes or states were you aware of at the time?
7. Have you shared all that is significant with reference to the experience?

BEGINNING AN INTERVIEW

Prior to the interview the primary investigator engages in the Epoche process described earlier so that, to a significant degree, past associations, understandings, "facts," biases, are set aside and do not color or direct the interview. Engaging in the Epoche process may also be necessary during the interview.

An example of beginning an interview is taken from Rick Copen's (1992) preliminary work on insomnia.

J = Janet
R = Rick

J: I don't know where. I'm not sure where you want me to start, how to get into this.

R: You can start by describing your experience with insomnia when it first occurred.

J: I still wake up in the middle of the night and I'll go through nights when I wake up and I can't get back to sleep, you know. All thoughts will run through my mind.

R: All thoughts like—

J: Well, concerns, my children. I think about my children and their younger days. I live a lot in the past.

R: Okay, those ruminations at night, they're about the past.

J: And, well the past leading to the future and now and I think about dying a lot. I have very erratic bedtime hours and, um I, you know, am going to the Sleep Disorders Clinic and trying to get me to where I go to bed at a regular time and get up at a regular time.

R: Yes.

J: I eliminate naps . . . when I don't wake up in the middle of the night I can get maybe three or four hours of sleep at night. I'm exhausted the next day and because I don't work now, you know. I'm retired I have the ability to go take a nap, which throws me off kilter again, as far as going to bed early.

R: Early is what time?

J: Like nine, or nine-thirty.

R: And then how long would you sleep?

J: Until about, oh, two.

R: And when you wake up, what's it like?

J: Oh, I'm a very restless sleeper. I'm always rolling over and looking at the clock. And one of my things I have turned the clock to the wall now. I don't find myself looking for the clock 'cause I know it's not there. . . . I don't get a good night's rest. I have dreams. I mean, it seems like every time I wake up I'll go to the bathroom or something. I'm dreaming and the only way I can get back to sleep is to try to get right back to bed and think of the dream and get myself back into it.

R: Oh. And that helps.

J: That's what I've been doing ever since I've been to the clinic.

R: So you focus on the dream you've had and where you've left off and somehow that—

J: I try to. I don't know whether I dreamed but when I wake up again or when I wake up when I turn, I mean, I'm always turning. I'm a very, very restless sleeper and I don't remember being this restless before.

R: ... When you wake up at 2:00 in the morning, are you wide awake then?

J: I am if I get in bed and start thinking. You know, if I start thinking, no matter what it is. I'll have something on my mind you know, and um, for, you know, and I'll start. If I think about anything in the present, my present life then I won't go back to sleep and I can get off on tangents and other thoughts and I'll stay awake for several hours.

R: You're waking up then is kind of a gradual thing at two in the morning? And then you'll start thinking?

J: When I wake up it must be when I turn over or when I look at the clock and if I start thinking of something immediately then. If I look and I see it's three thirty sometimes I'll think, oh, great. I'm going to be awake again. Or sometimes I'll think, Oh, I've only got two more hours before, you know. Then I'll start thinking. You know, it depends on how I feel about myself. You know, I'm extremely, my life seems to be centered around my weight, and if I'm thinner I feel better and I like myself. I've recently lost forty pounds through an Opti-Fast program, and I've put on ten of it. I don't like it. And so I'm upset and if I wake up in the middle of the night the first thing I think of, I go to the bathroom and I get on the scales in the middle of the night to see if I've lost any weight. [Reprinted by permission of the author]

ORGANIZATION AND ANALYSIS OF DATA

Organization of data begins when the primary researcher places the transcribed interviews before him or her and studies the material through the methods and procedures of phenomenal analysis. The procedures include *horizonalizing* the data and regarding every horizon or statement relevant to the topic and question as having equal value. From the horizonalized statements, the *meaning or meaning units* are listed. These are *clustered* into common categories or *themes,* removing overlapping and repetitive statements. The clustered themes and meanings are used to develop the *textural descriptions of the experience.* From the textural descriptions, structural descriptions and an integration of textures and structures into the meanings and essences of the phenomenon are constructed.

REFERENCES

Blanck, P. D., Bellack, A. S., Rosnow, R. L., Rotheram-Borus, M. J., & Schooler, N. R. (1992). Scientific rewards and conflicts of ethical choices in human subjects research. *American Psychologists, 47*(7), 959-965.

Cooper, H. (1989). *Integrating research: A guide for literature review.* Newbury Park, CA: Sage.

Copen, R. (1992). *Initial interview on the experience of insomnia.* Unpublished raw data.

Copen, R. (1993). Insomnia: A phenomenological investigation. (Doctoral dissertation, The Union Institute, 1992). *Dissertation Abstracts International, 53,* 6542B.

Fraelich, C. B. (1989). A phenomenological investigation of the psychotherapist's experience of presence. (Doctoral dissertation, The Union Institute, 1988). *Dissertation Abstracts International, 50,* 1643B.

Humphrey, E. (1991). Searching for life's meaning: A phenomenological and heuristic exploration of the experience of searching for meaning in life. (Doctoral dissertation, The Union Institute, 1992). *Dissertation Abstracts International, 51,* 4051B.

LaCourse, K. (1991). *The experience of time.* Unpublished manuscript, Center for Humanistic Studies, Detroit, MI.

Stevick, E. L. (1971). An empirical investigation of the experience of anger. In A. Giorgi, W. F. Fischer, & E. Von Eckartsberg (Eds.), *Duquesne studies in phenomenological psychology* (Vol. 1). Pittsburgh: Duquesne University Press.

Trumbull, M. (1993). The experience of undergoing coronary artery bypass surgery: A phenomenological investigation. (Doctoral dissertation, The Union Institute, 1993). *Dissertation Abstracts International, 54,* 1115B.

7

PHENOMENOLOGICAL RESEARCH
Analyses and Examples

This chapter presents methods of analysis of data and examples of research data derived from human science research investigations. To guide human science researchers, I have developed modifications of two methods of analysis of data. The first is my modification of van Kaam's (1959, 1966) method of analysis. Each of the steps in analyzing the transcribed interview of each research participant is included in the following outline.

MODIFICATION OF THE VAN KAAM METHOD OF ANALYSIS OF PHENOMENOLOGICAL DATA

Using the complete transcription of each research participant:

1. *Listing and Preliminary Grouping*
   List every expression relevant to the experience. (Horizonalization)
2. *Reduction and Elimination:* To determine the Invariant Constituents:
   Test each expression for two requirements:

    a. Does it contain a moment of the experience that is a necessary and sufficient constituent for understanding it?

    b. Is it possible to abstract and label it? If so, it is a horizon of the experience. Expressions not meeting the above requirements are eliminated. Overlapping, repetitive, and vague expressions are also eliminated or presented in more exact descriptive terms. The horizons that remain are the invariant constituents of the experience.

3. Clustering and Thematizing the Invariant Constituents:

    Cluster the invariant constituents of the experience that are related into a thematic label. The clustered and labeled constituents are the core themes of the experience.

4. Final Identification of the Invariant Constituents and Themes by Application: Validation

    Check the invariant constituents and their accompanying theme against the complete record of the research participant. (1) Are they expressed explicitly in the complete transcription? (2) Are they compatible if not explicitly expressed? (3) If they are not explicit or compatible, they are not relevant to the co-researcher's experience and should be deleted.

5. Using the relevant, validated invariant constituents and themes, construct for each co-researcher an *Individual Textural Description* of the experience. Include verbatim examples from the transcribed interview.

6. Construct for each co-researcher an *Individual Structural Description* of the experience based on the Individual Textural Description and Imaginative Variation.

7. Construct *for each research participant* a *Textural-Structural Description* of the meanings and essences of the experience, incorporating the invariant constituents and themes.

From the Individual Textural-Structural Descriptions, develop a Composite Description of the meanings and essences of the experience, representing the group as a whole.

MODIFICATION OF THE STEVICK-COLAIZZI-KEEN METHOD OF ANALYSIS OF PHENOMENOLOGICAL DATA

A second method of organizing and analyzing phenomenological data is derived from my modification of methods of analysis suggested by Stevick (1971), Colaizzi (1973), and Keen (1975). Each of the steps is presented in the appropriate order of analysis.

1. Using a phenomenological approach, obtain a full description of your own experience of the phenomenon.
2. From the verbatim transcript of your experience complete the following steps:
   a. Consider each statement with respect to significance for description of the experience.
   b. Record all relevant statements.
   c. List each nonrepetitive, nonoverlapping statement. These are the invariant horizons or meaning units of the experience.
   d. Relate and cluster the invariant meaning units into themes.
   e. Synthesize the invariant meaning units and themes into *a description of the textures of the experience*. Include verbatim examples.
   f. Reflect on your own textural description. Through imaginative variation, construct *a description of the structures of your experience*.
   g. Construct *a textural-structural description* of the meanings and essences of your experience.
3. From the verbatim transcript of the experience of *each* of the other *co-researchers*, complete the above steps, a through g.
4. From the individual textural-structural descriptions of all co-researchers' experiences, construct *a composite textural-structural description of the meanings and essences of the experience,* integrating all individual textural-structural descriptions into a universal description of the experience representing the group as a whole.

In the sections that follow, from various research investigations, I will offer examples of *Horizonalization; Delimiting to Invariant Horizons* or Meaning Units, *Clustering* the Invariant Constituents *into Themes, Individual* Textural and *Individual* Structural Descriptions, *Composite Textural* and *Composite Structural Descriptions,* and *Synthesis of Textural and Structural Meanings and Essences.*

Horizonalization: Fraelich's Study
of the Psychologist-Therapist's Presence

In this excerpt from a research interview (Fraelich, 1989), I have selected portions of the verbatim transcription, representing Horizonalization of the therapist's experience of "presence." This example of horizonalization illustrates the importance of being receptive to every statement of the co-researcher's experience, granting each comment equal value and thus encouraging a rhythmical flow between the research participant and researcher, interaction that inspires comprehensive disclosure of experience. The excerpt on the therapist's experience of presence begins with an open invitation. The research participant describes *presence* as inner preparation, internal awareness of space, and imaginative readiness as ways of entering into the therapeutic encounter, setting the tone, and conveying an alertness, receptiveness, and attunement to listening, hearing, and responding to whatever the person-in-therapy presents. Each statement in horizonalizing holds equal value and contributes to an understanding of the nature and meaning of therapist presence.

R = Researcher
P = Participant

R: What I'd like you to do is, as fully as possible, describe in your own words how you experience presence as a therapist. Would you just start with getting into that experience. . . . Take your time; when you're ready, begin.

P: Well, when you read the description of presence . . . I realized that one of the things I do—I try to do—like if I'm seeing a number of people, is to have enough space in-between so that there's some kind of preparation beforehand. This is more an inner preparation. The fellow I'm thinking of comes once a week. Before he comes, I first of all just take a look at the notes from the week before. Not so much to catch up on the details but just to kind of bring him present to me. Then when I've done that, I picture him in his situation, especially as described there, and I just kind of take that in so I feel I begin presence already. Just taking him into my consciousness before he comes. So that's one aspect.

R: . . . kind of a preparation, setting a tone.

P: Setting of a tone that puts me in relationship to him and . . . where I'm just bringing everything to rest. You know, if I've been working all morning long, or been in conversation with somebody just trying to let all that drop away so that I can have as open a consciousness as possible.

R: So the outside world gets put away.

P: Yes, just leave that behind. The kind of preparation for just being there with him.

R: Do you have any other experience that's a part of this preparation time?

P: Well, no I don't. When I take a look at the notes I've taken from last week, I try to get a sense of what we left off talking about. . . . I try to tune in on what we ended up with. And I'll usually make reference to that as the first thing to begin.

R: So you try to beforehand just before the session, just as you enter, you try to get in touch as much as possible with where the person's been, where they're kind of at at the moment, where they're going toward, you try to get a sense of that.

P: That's part of it. I realize there's also a sense, and this is part of my preparation, that even though I have that in mind, I also want to be really open just to where he is now when he walks in the room. And that may be very different than in the last session a week ago, whenever it was.

R: It's an openness, just a letting be quality . . . trying to get a sense of where he is.

P: I want to be open to where he's at. I'm dropping all my thoughts, coming to a quiet state of consciousness. It's important so that I can just take in the new, you know, as though it were the first time I was seeing him, with some sense of wondering what he's going to bring . . . it definitely feels like presence or the presencing of myself.

R: Now, I have a fairly clear sense of what that's like for you. You're wanting to be close to the person. You're ready and there waiting for him.

P: Yes, you're right.

R: Can you tell me more about what it's like?

P: Well, it's like wanting to know and caring about who he is. It comes to me as a kind of question that I don't know who he is. It's like he's presented his life story or whatever parts of it; he's described a lot about himself, and within that it's a kind of riddle, it's like there's a lot of unfinished business, there's a lot of themes that are more implicit than explicit. And so it's kind of questioning, "Bill, who really is this person, who is this struggling, individual manifesting his various feelings and thoughts, experiences of life. Who is really there?"

R: Which is interest and concern?

P: Yeah. Caring about him, caring about where he's going, that I've made an alliance with him. I've taken on some kind of responsibility for helping him get a sense of who he is and where he's going.

R: Also, there seems to be that wondering—I wonder what this person's about.

P: Yeah. . . . I just wonder what's back of there. I think to the extent in which one has a heightened interest you know, you get results. You either insert yourself in there to experience, say the other person's world, and that's where I think the interest is, it brings us into another person's world. . . . Psychotherapy for me is immersing myself in the world of the other as much as possible. That's part of dropping my own world as a preparation for the session. To drop it that so that I can be free. . . . I can sit there and muse about what I'm going to be doing in an hour or what I've been doing the hour beforehand, or I can let that go and get in touch with my concerns and his anxieties, and really just focus, really enter that other person's world.

R: It sounds like you direct your concern to him but still being there with you, bringing yourself in, leaving your own concerns.

P: Leaving my own concerns, my own thoughts, my own feeling about myself, my work, play, whatever. It's up to him to bring what he wants. He has to decide that, to bring that, bring part of himself and I want to be there as a kind of a guest. For me that's kind of a good image. Ready your house or whatever before a guest comes. You're thinking about the guest, getting ready, and you're there for him.

R: You mentioned heightened awareness. Could you say more about that?

P: Well, heightened I guess in the sense of full, heightened in the sense of finely tuned. Well, I get the image again maybe having my thoughts and feelings going out in various directions of my life, I'm pulling that energy that's taking me to other concerns in my life and pulling that energy into myself and directing it into the interest and receptivity towards my client—so that I'm awake, having a heightened consciousness. Just kind of a fullness of being there. (Fraelich, 1989, pp. 87-95) [Reprinted by permission of the author]

Horizonalization: Palmieri's Study of Child Abuse

A second example of horizonalization is taken from Palmieri's (1990) investigation of "The Experience of Adults Abused as Children." His interview with Geraldine illustrates the first step of phenomenological analysis—horizonalization or recognition that every statement has equal value. The following horizonal statements are excerpted from the first fifth and last fifth of the research interview with Geraldine in which she recounts her experience of being sexually abused as a child by her father. Each horizon of the research interview adds meaning and provides an increasingly clear portrayal of scenes of sexual abuse, the unfolding situation in which the abuse occurs, and the thoughts and feelings of the victim.

First Fifth of the Interview

1. "I remember the door and was standing in between the door to the living room and the kitchen and my dad approaching me very gently."

2. "I'm feeling, I can feel real tense, resisting, but yet having no control over the situation at all."

3. "I think I was entering the kitchen from the living room and my dad came up from behind me, from the living room. He was sitting in his chair before that."

4. "And, as I walked into the living room he kinda caught me right then. And, just continued to perform *that* on me. Staring at me the whole time. Yeah, with him down on his knees, just staring up at me the whole time."

5. "I just remember his eyes. I never saw hate in them. It was just like a longing. Like a need for something. I don't know. At the time I didn't know what it was."

6. "But now, after being married, I would maybe refer to it as some kind of sexual longing. Passionate. I was afraid. A little nervous. A little shaky."

7. "I remember thinking back. There was nobody home and I wondered if anyone was going to walk in at the time, being the fact that it was right in the middle of the house in a wide open area. If anyone were to enter from either doorway, they would see."

8. "Then in another way hoping someone would come home. Wondering where my brother was. Wondering where my sister was. How long they may be gone. When they might be coming home. That's what I remember thinking of."

9. "Hoping someone would just come in and stop it."

10. "I remember just pulling up my pants and just running into the bathroom. After it was over, all I could remember was just wanting to go to the bathroom and fixing myself up."

11. "I remember leaving the house and staying gone for quite a while until I noticed that someone was home again."

12. "I don't remember having any thoughts or feelings about my dad, though. All I can remember is escape and avoiding him. As far as any hatred towards him I never really realized that until just recently."

13. "I found out later on just a few years back that it happened to my sister too. . . . My dad's the one that told me. It's been brought up in therapy with my mom sitting in the room."

14. "Thinking back now, I know from being in therapy and talking to others that it wasn't my fault. But, I can't remember at the time if I felt it was my fault or not. I don't remember that at all."

15. "All I can remember is trying, doing anything and everything in my power to avoid him so it wouldn't happen again. I was always watching him."

16. "I felt that he was looking right through me. I felt very uncomfortable when he looked at me. I just remember avoiding him so much that even when I'd get those looks, I'd feel so uncomfortable. And when he'd look, it would seem like just that he knows something, or that he's done something that I felt was wrong." (Palmieri, 1990, pp. 50-52) [Reprinted by permission of the author]

Last Fifth of the Interview

1. "One word does come to mind, shame. Feeling shamed, I was shamed. My dad was shaming me. Made me feel dirty."

2. "I mean at the time being just twelve years old, at a time when I should have been just starting to grow and learn about sexuality through my own experiences . . . my own . . . what I wanted to do . . . not just being forced to do something. And I feel he just took that all away from me."

3. "Because after that happened, I just didn't, my feelings towards men and boys in general, just changed. I was just starting to like boys at the time."

4. "I don't know. I think my perception of what sexual relationships were supposed to be . . . they weren't that way for me at all. Like even with this great sexual relationship with Jason. It wasn't what I had dreamt it would be. Just something romantic, storybook type fantasies of being totally desirable and accepted the way I am. And not expecting any more out of me than what I was willing to give. Those types of fantasies."

5. "I feel it with Ron. Well, for one thing Ron's very understanding. He's very gentle. But, then over the years now mine and Ron's relationship was real good at first; and then kind of like for the last five, six years when all this surfaced with me, and just being in therapy in and out, it hasn't been so good. But, then lately it's been good again. It's been kind of back and forth."

6. "I mean Ron has never tried to force me or coerce me to do anything that I didn't want to do. Where with my dad, all of that was totally against my wish. I respected Ron for that because he wasn't after me just for sex; which is what I felt from my dad."

7. "I know what scared me the most was mainly with my oldest daughter . . . she's going to be ten and starting to develop. That's a strong fear of the same thing happening to her that happened to me."

8. "At first I thought from her dad because it happened to me from my dad. But, then I'm thinking Ron could never do that. That's what I mean. Part of me saying he could never do that because I think I know this man well enough; but then, my mom evidently knew my dad. I really don't believe my mom knew what was going on."

9. "I talked to Ron and he knows what happened to me. I really, ninety-nine percent of me is sure that he would never touch his daughter, but there's still that 1 percent cautious."

10. "I do talk to Carrie a lot about it. Just about the subject itself and just letting her know that if anyone touches her no matter who it is, that she, you know, can come to me."

11. "And she has come to me. She's been approached by one of her girlfriend's fathers. And I wanted to go down there and strangle him. But, she didn't want me. She didn't even want me to talk to him about it."
12. "For a long time I think I blamed my mom for what my dad did to me. Because of the fact it happened to her. She was sexually abused by her dad. And if she was sexually abused by her dad and I was by my dad . . . makes me more in tune with my daughter's feelings, needs . . . what signs to look for."
13. "Then I wonder why she wasn't seeing what was going on. Even in just the way it changed me." (Palmieri, 1990, pp. 52-54) [Reprinted by permission of the author]

Invariant Horizons or Constituents: Suspicion

The invariant horizons point to the unique qualities of an experience, those that stand out. De Koning (1979) reduced the experience of one co-researcher's description of suspicion to the following core horizons in which the conditions of suspicion arise, the clues of suspicion are recognized, and the suspicion itself is validated or shown to be unfounded.

1. I was in a situation where I did not feel insecure, but knew I could easily be so, as I had done on a similar occasion. I was with a married couple and a friend.
2. The married couple related very well with each other and the friend (of which I was slightly envious). They had known each other for some time and I was the newcomer into the group. I was on intimate terms with only one member of the group and had known the married couple for only a short time.
3. Their reputation for relating well preceded them, but I had experienced it very strongly as well on the occasions that I met them.
4. I felt as if my ability to communicate well was being observed and (perhaps) tested.
5. I felt this particularly strongly as the couple were very fond of the third member of the trio (my friend) and I was the "new woman" in his life; I felt that my whole performance was being judged.
6. Especially remembering what had been said about the previous girlfriend and thinking about being "found lacking" in some respect in their eyes.
7. The female half of the couple has a very powerful personality and the other partner can be painfully direct in both his questions and statements, as I had already unfortunately discovered.

8. During the course of the evening, I had already had the feeling that something had been said about me by the female half of the couple, as indeed I had experienced once before, but had never actually discovered whether I was in fact correct in my assumption that something "unkind" had been said about me in my presence.

9. On this third occasion I doubted that even this couple, with their reputation for directness, would say something while I was there, but at the same time I felt sure that a comment had been made very quietly and quickly.

10. I began to wonder what I had done or said that might have provoked a disapproving comment. I quickly relived the events and conversations that had passed, also wondering if it might not be an isolated ill-judged statement on my part that provoked her response, but a more general feeling that would make them say something about me.

11. I also could not decide whether to challenge them about it, as, if I was wrong, my whole insecurity would be exposed, which would detract from my sense of relief, plus the fact that I would have to apologize for thinking that they had been "nasty."

12. I also had the feeling that if I was right, I might not want to know what it was that they disliked about me.

13. In the end, I did challenge them, which took a fair bit of courage on my part. It turned out that I was in fact wrong, but I was right in my feeling that my sense of relief was not all that it might have been, because now everyone knew that I had (unfounded) suspicions about their feelings towards me.

14. I suppose I was particularly sensitive, as having their approval of me would have meant quite a lot and I knew that their opinions were respected by my friend.

15. At the time when I thought something had been said, I felt something stir in my stomach and a rush of adrenaline run round my body, as if I might have to defend myself from their assumed attack.

16. I was not immediately convinced that my suspicions were totally without foundation, as, even if nothing had actually been said, I wondered if something in their manner, or the inflection in their voices might be saying just as much as actual words.

17. Only much later did I become convinced that nothing against me had been said and did I feel relieved." (De Koning, 1979, pp. 125-127) [Reprinted by permission of Duquesne University Press.]

Invariant Constituents or Horizons: Bypass Surgery

Trumbull (1993) analyzed the verbatim transcripts of all 14 of his co-researchers' experiences of undergoing coronary artery bypass surgery in order to determine the significant, relevant, and invariant meanings that provide living descriptions or highlights of the experience. He derived 44 invariant constituents and clustered them into eight themes, as follows:

I. Relationships with Medical Personnel, Information, Process, and Interventions
   A. Relationships with medical staff
   B. The first signs and symptoms of the development of heart problems
   C. Undergoing a series of medical tests
   D. The cost of coronary artery bypass surgery
   E. Being informed by the medical staff about the events, test and procedures
   F. Thoughts and memories and actually hearing of the surgical procedure
   G. The medical preparations that were necessary for coronary artery bypass surgery

II. Bodily Pain and Concerns Related to CABG Surgery
   A. Waking up after surgery with tubes protruding from one's body
   B. Being extremely thirsty but only allowed minimal amount of fluids
   C. The recovery process at home
   D. Involvement in exercise programs and developing regular exercise
   E. Perception of time as healer
   F. Chest pain
   G. Incision
   H. Leg pain
   I. Fear of continued heart problems and possible heart attack or having to undergo coronary artery bypass surgery again
   J. Regaining body functions after surgery
   K. Increased awareness of one's heart, and exercise, diet
   L. Being hooked up to machines
   M. Return to one's usual activities
   N. Hallucinations
   O. An awareness of the co-researcher's improvement after having coronary artery bypass surgery

III. Feelings and Memories Connected to the Surgery
   A. Disbelief that the co-researcher was experiencing heart problems that required heart surgery
   B. Feelings about how the physician and medical personnel took control of the person's life

C. Anticipating the surgery

D. Increased awareness of feelings

E. The negative impact of surgery

F. Feeling vulnerable

G. Feeling that life or God or the world was unjust in that they should have heart problems

H. Dealing with the physical pain

I. A sense that the person has lost control of what was happening to him or her

J. A feeling of being safe in the hospital

K. Last memories just prior to having heart bypass surgery

L. First memories after surgery

IV. Significance of Family and Friends

A. Relationships with family members

B. Relationships with friends

V. Impact of Time on Undergoing CABG Surgery

A. Perception of time

B. Experiences that remind the individual of earlier times

VI. Visions of Death Connected to CABG Surgery

A. Thoughts of one's own death

VII. Awakening or Confirming Religious Beliefs

A. Impact of surgery on the individual's religious beliefs

VIII. Horizons of New Life Following CABG Surgery

A. Importance or meaning of the surgery

B. A sense of new life

C. Making diet changes

D. Changing smoking habits. (Trumbull, 1993, pp. 121-122) [Reprinted by permission of the author]

Thematic Portrayal:
Miesel's Study of Midlife Career Change

From the invariant constituents, the researcher, using phenomenological reflection and imaginative variation, constructs thematic portrayals of the experience. Miesel (1991) studied "the experience of changing one's career during midlife." The following verbatim excerpts represent his clustering of the delimited meanings or horizons into core themes. They represent distinctive processes that are inherent in and often sequences of midlife career change.

1. *Effects of personal perceptions on the change process*—The data reveal that three main factors influenced participants' personal perceptions: (1) the magnitude of the changer's self-esteem; (2) the presence of support from significant others; and (3) the personal meanings derived from cultivating life events. These factors accounted in large part for individual differences in how they came to view the transition and what it meant in their lives.

2. *Core feelings and bodily awareness*—Intense feelings were generated by the conflict established by the decision-making process. Ensuing doubts and fears were often accompanied by specific bodily reactions. Negative feelings were replaced by hope and personal satisfaction as the process unfolded.

3. *Career change and self-actualization*—Career changers were growth-oriented and interested in reaching toward their highest potential. As they struggled with the process, they revealed needs for achievement, creativity and self-expression in their work. Nine out of twelve of the participants returned to school for training in their new careers. Strong references were made regarding the decision, difficulties, successes and personal meanings inherent in that portion of the transition. Money and time were powerful factors that needed to be dealt with.

4. *The integration of a new identity*—Voluntary midlife career redirection becomes a vehicle to identify more of one's authentic self. Hidden aspects of a person's personality rise to the surface as new needs are created and met. This process is ongoing and an integral part of the experience as one continues to interact with his or her new career and its perceived meanings. There is a "transition period" that the changer passes through as he or she takes on the new career identity.

5. *Refocusing of personal values*—At specific points in the transition, changers engaged in an internal dialogue regarding how they felt about themselves and the direction that they were going. Some of the old values were dropped or altered. New ones moved to a more prominent position. These changes appeared to create different effects depending on the way in which the changers chose to deal with the transition, their gender, or how they viewed the value of education and personal growth.

6. *Influence of time and space*—These entities were combined into one embracing theme which contained universal structures and multidimensional qualities. Time was experienced in a linear and existential form. Space was initially experienced in confining ways which tended to open up to a sense of freedom in the latter phases of the experience.

7. *Effects on relationship to self and others*—Career change influenced the relationship with others, particularly one's spouse. Meaningful change transpired in relationships that were open, honest and supportive. The change propelled the participants into looking more deeply at themselves and their lives as they progressed. They were able to break down internal barriers and identify new career goals. The meanings derived for women were in many respects different than those for men. Women indicated that their schooling and career transition filled a void that had been created by the absence of children and resultant purpose in life. The women in the study felt comfortable competing with men. Special problems often surfaced as roles changed in the household and new stresses emerged.

8. *Incorporation of new learnings*—Changers indicated that the change had positively reinforced their ability to get what they needed from life. Numerous references were made in regard to the discovery of a deeper sense of self and life purpose that was primarily obtained through new educational opportunities and life experiences. Many changers expressed the desire to continue their learning while engaged in their new careers. (Miesel, 1991, pp. 102-114) [Reprinted by permission of the author]

Individual Textural Description: Copen's Study of Insomnia

From the themes and delimited horizons of each research participant's experience, a textural description is constructed. Copen (1993) investigated insomnia through lengthy interviews with 10 research participants who had referred themselves to a sleep disorder clinic in East Lansing, MI. From the verbatim transcribed interviews of each co-researcher, he developed an individual textural description of the experience of insomnia. The following selection presents the nature and focus of the experience of insomnia, as narrated by Jim. I have selected this excerpt because it evokes clear images of what happens during insomnia, the thoughts, feelings, and struggles of the person who desperately wants to sleep but is unable to do so.

Textural Description of Jim's Insomnia

The experience of insomnia for Jim is one of restless fluctuation from an initial falling asleep to a sudden awakening. Wanting desperately to sleep but to no avail, he is "propelled into being awake"; imprisoned by wakefulness. This kind of being awake is powerful and charged with distress. "It's like being plugged in or amped . . . bug eyed." The growing fatigue becomes every bit as confining as the wakefulness. Sleep is nowhere to be found; there is just this experience of being "simultaneously fatigued, mentally and physically, but absolutely wide awake."

Time during sleep hours becomes a major concern. "I'm always rolling over and looking at the clock."

The night is experienced as both long and short. "I don't think the morning's ever far in the future. It's always much too close. What's long is the turmoil and the wrestling. . . . Trying to cope with it . . . but morning is always on you!"

Time in the waking world in also of concern. There isn't enough time to do what needs to be done. Time is always "running and no quiet time and no special time to get off and to abstract into obscure areas of interest and putz around."

Eventually, poor sleep habits develop and lead to an irregular sleep schedule. "I just started staying up later . . . it's really hard to decelerate, when you're running."

The nightly companionship of insomnia is comprised of feelings of anxiety, panic and worrisome thoughts, especially thoughts about not being able to sleep. "I'd be thinking about work . . . personal affairs . . . my mind would just churn and churn . . . churning and ruminating and perseverating . . . I was obsessing."

Tormented by negative thoughts and worry about possible health problems left Jim shaken and became the legacy of night after night of restless turmoil.

During the insomnia the consequences of not sleeping stood out sharply "like skyscrapers on the horizon of a large city." Memories of sleepless nights were brought to awareness the next day, a day in which he would be "wretched, feeling demented, feeling damned, feeling burned out." "It's like being sick with the flu . . . it's just awful, negative, jarring." Repeatedly, the wave would arise within him, the piercing knowledge that by not sleeping, the next day "will be hellish. Your body will be crying out for sleep and your brain will be numb." Eventually, following day after day of not sleeping, self-confidence is severely damaged. "It's so ungodly . . . it's like a waste. It's like everything takes so much energy, energy that you don't have, it's like being consumed . . . it's kind of like dying."

Jim's experience of insomnia contains four core textural themes that precipitate and account for his dilemma of not being able to fall asleep: 1) thoughts that interfere with sleep; 2) feelings that interfere with sleep; 3) restless and anxious time; and 4) disturbing consequences of insomnia.

The erratic fluctuation of quick sleep followed by sudden awakening evokes catastrophic struggles of Jim in relation to himself. He's "plugged in," "amped," "bug eyed" and simultaneously exhausted and wide awake. The consequences of insomnia become feared and provide fuel to the troubling thoughts and feelings that keep sleep at bay. (Copen, 1993, pp. 58-60) [Reprinted by permission of the author]

Individual Textural Description: Aanstoos's Study of Being Left Out

Aanstoos (1987) obtained vivid descriptions of the experience of being left out from 25 research participants, who were students in three different classes. The following is Sarah's description of being left out. The excerpt that follows, briefly but effectively captures the situation, conditions, and relationship in which feeling left out occurs.

Sarah's Description of Being Left Out

On a bright summer afternoon my sister came home from college with her boyfriend. That night she told me they were going to get married that November. I went to my room and did not come out the rest of the night. My sister and I had been very close. She always petted me. She is a year older than I. But she had nothing to say to me the rest of the weekend. She did not talk to me. It was as if I were not there. When she returned to school I felt as if she hadn't really been home—it has been a bad dream. This was the way it was every time she came until the week of the wedding. She returned home Wednesday before the approaching Saturday wedding. It got worse Friday night before the rehearsal. I felt that no one cared if I were there or not, so I left, I came home late but they were having a party. It was after midnight (go to bed). I was very lonely and there was a house full of people. I was invisible to my sister. (Aanstoos, 1987, p. 154)

Individual Structural Descriptions of Insomnia

Copen (1993) constructed individual *structural* descriptions of the insomnia experience of each of his co-researchers.

The individual *structural* description provides a vivid account of the underlying dynamics of the experience, the themes and qualities that account for "how" feelings and thoughts connected with insomnia are aroused, what conditions evoke insomnia. Copen emphasizes that, "The structures are brought into the researcher's awareness through imaginative variation, reflection and analysis, beyond the appearance and into the real meanings or essences of the experience" (p. 65). Jim provides the data for Copen's individual structural description of the experience of insomnia, the most significant of which is the self in relation to time, obsessions with reference to time that stretch time and evoke anxiety and restlessness in the insomniac.

Structural Description of Jim's Insomnia

The structures that permeate Jim's insomnia and evoke penetrating and disturbing thoughts and feelings are expressed in Jim's relation to time, his relations with others, work habits, and sense of responsibility.

Regarding Self in relation to time, Jim is attuned to filling time with activity both during his waking hours and during his periods of insomnia. Time during insomnia is experienced both as too lengthy and too brief. He is often conscious of time moving ever so slowly while lying entangled in fears, obsessive thoughts and concerns of not having enough hours of sleep to cope with the next day. During those moments Jim is painfully aware of time moving by with rapidity, as morning rushes forth like a train. "It's rushing towards you . . . it's endless, you look at the clock and you realize your margin of getting it together is narrower and narrower." Time during Jim's waking hours is insufficient for inner reflection and awareness of its meaningfulness. He describes his days as having "no time to catch your breath."

In general, Jim's daylight time is filled with work, his nighttime with restlessness and worry. Moments of leisure or free time are not in the realm of his immediate possibilities. He is aware that somehow the insomnia has a stronghold [sic] on him and is related to his work habits and his sense of responsibility. When speaking of his insomnia, he exclaimed that work is the answer. "I really think work is it. I think work is basically it."

For Jim, Self in Relation to Others involves demands. As a social worker for a large agency, his caseload is overwhelming. He struggles to provide services to many individuals who need more than he can give. When he returns home in the evening, his son pulls at him in a needful manner. Jim describes coming home as the work of a "second shift." He is tired, and filled with frustration after putting in an arduous day, coupled with feeling exhausted from no sleep the night before. Jim's family, his only intimate relationships, are bounded by his sense of duty and his concern for their well-being.

Self in Relation to Work is a force projecting outwardly, described by Jim as every moment filled with activity and busyness. His sleeping hours are filled with worrisome thoughts and concerns much like his daily work schedule. Day or night there is no time for solitude or sanctuary in which he is the center of life, no room for becoming aware of his inner thoughts, feelings and possibilities.

Jim's insomnia is a metaphor for his existence. A chronically restless time, a time of worry devoid of self-reflection or contemplation. His sleep time is heavy with cognitive activity that prevents sleep. Often, Jim describes himself as burned-out, "I'm just somebody who's burned out, doing social work."

The implication is that Jim is lost. Even in insomnia concerns for others are the foci. There is no Self presence or being. He has ignored his own needs, wants and wishes, his innermost Self, and is out of touch with his potential for Self renewal and enrichment of inner life. Consequently, the insomnia mirrors his inability to renew spirit, mind, and body. (Copen, 1993, pp. 65-67) [Reprinted by permission of the author]

Buckley (1971) studied the phenomenology of at-homeness. In his investigation he explored situations of moving from one home to another that awakened feelings and thoughts of what it means to be at-home. Buckley offers the following individual structural description of the experience. I consider it a distinctive example of understanding the underlying structures that account for an experience being what it is.

Structural Description of Being at Home

A good part of feeling at home has to do with the satisfaction and security that comes from being in a situation which is *familiar,* that is, being situated within a *structure* that one knows about ahead of time and knows reasonably well what to expect, and knows this in a relatively unthreatened and comfortable manner. This is probably why it is also natural to think of at-homeness as being a sort of "at-easeness," which can be contrasted to dis-ease or undue experience of stress—or in a sense of feeling of relaxation and rest in the presence of the customary, the expected and the accepting. Another aspect on a somewhat deeper and more dynamic level is the feeling "I am where I can be myself," such as we feel on a largely behavioral level when there is no need to explain our actions to anyone or no need to feel on guard towards the misperceptions of the other, as, for example, when getting home tired in the late afternoon, I "feel free" to kick off my shoes and lie down flat on my back in the middle of the living room and close my eyes. (Buckley, 1971, p. 205)

Composite Textural Description

From the total group of individual textural descriptions the Composite Textural Description is developed. The invariant meanings and themes of every co-researcher are studied in depicting the experiences of the group as a whole.

Two clear and vivid examples of the Composite Textural Description have been selected to illustrate the composite textural description.

Humphrey's (1991) Composite Textural Description: Search for Life's Meanings

Childhood was a time of innocence. Immersed in family and religious belief systems, my research participants did not search consciously for life's meaning despite facing inner turmoil and crises. There was a general sense of acceptance and giving over to the authority's established meanings and plan for their life.

Then at some point or points in childhood or adolescence, every co-researcher experienced a growing awareness or awakening in which unquestioned beliefs were shaken. The process of differentiating a sense of life's meaning was launched. These experiences usually occurred in conjunction with feelings of fear, confusion, shock, loneliness, disillusionment and often self-blame or self-contempt. Participants felt separate, withdrawn or alienated and were unable to find or avoided finding anyone with whom to share their feelings.

For certain individuals a breakdown occurred in adolescence in some significant relationship to an external—family or religious—structure. Problems which had been simmering unconsciously for years and allegiances to particular authorities or belief systems which had been maintained but no longer were effective suddenly became clear to the participants. They experienced new dimensions of meaning, autonomy and vitality. Oppressive conditions gave way in the face of new insights and freedoms. Common feelings prior to the "breakdowns" were anger, bitterness and resentment, and, following the event, greater personal freedom and self-responsibility.

Co-researchers in their adult life often achieved the original goals they had accepted or set for themselves, sometimes experiencing temporary high points, only to discover that these did not bring happiness or fulfillment. In fact, the emptiness or sense of missing something after attaining . . . objectives made it more clear that the promise of an original life "program" was illusory.

For many participants there were singular events in adolescence or adulthood during which major changes in their sense of themselves and their world occurred. These breakthrough experiences were not consciously pursued but emerged as a much larger or deeper dimension out of what otherwise might have been an ordinary or normal event. The common feeling tones of these experiences include the excitement of discovery, heightened awareness of consciousness, a sense of intuitive knowing and clarity, expanding or opening, joy, a sense of certainty and strength, and feeling deeply and powerfully connected to life.

External catalysts, notably psychotherapy and drugs, were important for many participants in their initial searches for meaning. As young adults or adults, the research participants reported feeling depressed or in crisis as they began therapy, and then feeling more vulnerable, aware and open as their therapeutic work progressed. Drugs, especially LSD, were utilized by some participants in the drug-experimenting years of the late 1960s and early 1970s as a catalyst during the early phases of their search for meaning, providing a sense of new, mystical or fresh perspectives involving a dissolving or disordering of the ego, concepts and belief systems. Virtually none of the participants use drugs and very few use alcohol or tobacco now, preferring safer means of achieving deepening awareness and higher consciousness.

For other participants, their openings came as a result of crises which may have happened suddenly or developed over time. Unlike breakthrough experiences, crises usually were accompanied by significant emotional or physical distress, sometimes painful feelings of being sad, angry or frustrated, shocked, lost, hopeless, powerless, lonely or deeply questioning.

A wide range of participants' emotional expressions were described as intrinsic to search for meaning, from being isolated or separate from others or life to feeling connected, internally and/or externally. Loneliness, alienation, not fitting-in, being withdrawn and being different were feelings frequently expressed by participants in describing times in their lives when they felt alienated and disconnected. On the other hand, co-researchers also found enjoyment and a sense of mastery in searching and being alone. In contrast, feelings of joy, aliveness and being unified or centered were mentioned in conjunction with feeling connected with life.

Participants mentioned that there is a dark side to their search, fear or terror of facing an existential vacuum, in some cases provoked by death or monumental world problems. Sometimes the awareness of time and life passing quickly brought strong feelings of fear or terror. Feelings of hopelessness, helplessness, despair and meaninglessness also were mentioned. The possibility that the universe is essentially chaotic and without meaning brought feelings of emptiness, being lost or overwhelmed, an almost unbearable darkness. The intensity of this fear of the existential void may help to explain why some participants suspect that they are reticent to question their existing belief systems.

Often during searches for meaning, discovery took the form of "This Is It!"—lasting from a few moments to several days. Feelings associated with this state included a sense of certainty, being filled up, joy, peacefulness and a feeling that everything was perfect or fit correctly.

For many participants a deep sense of inner peace and connectedness was a goal sometimes achieved in their search for meaning. Their descriptions of these experiences were powerful and filled with awe and wonder.

Research participants generally described feelings ranging from excitement to passion. . . . Often they acknowledged that they were unable to articulate a finite meaning, but experienced a felt clarity or certainty in pursuing what they believed to be meaningful. Many participants related their search for meaning to their sense of a life task. Inspired by their searching and what they already had found, they describe the search as inspirational, exciting and ongoing. (Humphrey, 1991, pp. 124-129) [Reprinted by permission of the author]

The second illustration of a Composite Textural Description is excerpted from Yoder's (1990) study of guilt. The most telling quality of guilt is in relationship to self, a divided self, struggling with feelings of doubt, self-rejection, and life in an alien world.

Yoder's Composite Textural Description of Feeling Guilty

The experience of feeling guilty is felt as an intense and permeating reality. Everything else fades in comparison. The feeling of guilt immediately severs the connections between the individual and the world of other people. Perhaps the most telling ingredient is the felt split from one's own self.

The world, for the one experiencing guilt feelings, is an alien world—a being in limbo, with unreal and cloudy forms dimly perceived. Pain is the one central reality. The person immersed in guilt goes through the motions of living but moves and acts without thought, automatically, like a robot.

The inhabitants of the everyday world are strangers who have no place in the world of guilt. Talking to others is useless since they would not understand. The danger of criticism and judgment is ever present. The person when feeling guilty struggles to hide the feeling from the outside world, especially when condemnation is anticipated.

The most painful aspects of feeling guilty are related to the self. When feeling guilty, the individual experiences alienation. He or she stands apart and, with disgust and disdain, views the self as other. At the same time, there is the clear realization that the observing self is the one viewed. This often leads to self-rejection and self-hatred. In guilt feelings, one punishes oneself, sometimes drastically. The perception of self is changed in the experience of guilt feelings. Positive aspects are perceived as unreal and without substance. Confidence deteriorates to insecurity, attractiveness to ugliness, and competence to inadequacy.

At the same time the individual perceives himself or herself to be basically good, a nice person. This produces confusion, turmoil, self-doubting. "How could I have done that?" The person is not the one he or she wants to be. Self-standards and judgments have deteriorated. There is no escape from guilt feelings. They are obsessive. Although the individual is acutely aware that the guilty act cannot be undone, torturing thoughts of "what if" plague the participant. When there is a choice between self and others or between one possible course of action and another, there is also a realization that no option works because the feelings of guilt are inevitable.

An integral part of the experience of feeling guilty is the belief that the individual has the ability and power to make choices and decisions and is, therefore, responsible for the outcome. Linked to this is the desire to be in control. The battle rages within, between the desire to escape from the pain and the wanting to believe in one's power to act in a new way. The individual begins to question the self endlessly, like a computer trying to find the answer to an unanswerable question.

Other painful emotions are experienced. Guilt feelings cut into happiness and turn it to shame, fear, anxiety, and an inconsolable feeling of loss. The world falls apart. The person is angry and the anger is directed against the self.

Physical sensations are intense and varied. In some cases, the body is experienced as alien. . . . The feeling of guilt is described as stomach butterflies, intestines tied in knots. It is hot, searing, sharp, and tearing. The person feels flushed. There is often a constriction in the throat. Breathing is shallow. Tears flow easily.

Sometimes guilty memories return suddenly, springing up with a jolt. At other times, they emerge slowly, painfully, haltingly. The feeling of guilt comes in waves, crushes, and weighs heavily, endlessly on the one who feels guilty. (Yoder, 1990, pp. 102-105) [Reprinted by permission of the author.]

Composite Structural Description

The next process of phenomenological analysis employs Imaginative Variation. From the Composite Textural Description of each research participant, and use of Imaginative Variation, a Composite Structural Description, representing the group of co-researchers as a whole, is constructed.

The Composite Structural Description is a way of understanding *how* the co-researchers as a group experience *what* they experience. I have selected two examples from phenomenological investigations to illustrate the *Composite Structural Description*. The Fischer and Wertz (1979) report portrays the themes and essences in living descriptions that enable one to know the meaning of criminal victimization from the internal perceptions and images of the victim.

Composite Structural Description:
Fischer and Wertz Study of Being Criminally Victimized

In their report of an empirical phenomenological analysis of being criminally victimized, Fischer and Wertz (1979) present the following Composite Structural Description of the experience:

Being criminally victimized is a disruption of daily routine. It is a disruption that compels one, despite resistance, to face one's fellow as predator and oneself as prey, even though all the while anticipating consequences, planning, acting, and looking to others for assistance. These efforts to little avail, one experiences vulnerability, separateness, and helplessness in the face of the callous, insensitive, often anonymous enemy. Shock and disbelief give way to puzzlement, strangeness, and then to a sense of the crime as perverse, unfair, undeserved. Whether or not expressed immediately, the victim experiences a general inner protest, anger or rage, and a readiness for retaliation, for revenge against the violator.

As life goes on, the victim finds him/herself pervasively attuned to the possibility of victimization—through a continued sense of reduced agency, of the other as predatory, and of community as inadequately supportive. More particularly, one continues to live the victimization through recollections of the crime, imagination of even worse outcomes, vigilant suspiciousness of others, sensitivity to news of disorder and crime, criticalness of justice system agents, and desires to make sense of it all.

But these reminders of vulnerability are simultaneously efforts toward recovery of independence, safety, trust, order, and sense. One begins to get back on top of the situation through considering or taking precautions against crime, usually by restricting one's range of activities so as not to fall prey again. During this process, the victim tries to understand not only how a criminal could have done and could again do such a thing, but also how he or she (the victim) may have contributed to the criminal's action. Also, one's intermittent readiness for retaliation provides a glimpse of one's own potential for outrageous violence. The victim thus is confronted with the paradoxical and ambiguous character of social existence: the reversible possibilities we all share, such as being agent or object, same or different, disciplined or disruptive, predator or prey. One may move from this encounter to a more circumspect attitude toward personal responsibility. However, the person's efforts toward such an integration of the victimization are not sufficient. The environment must over time demonstrate that the victim's extreme vigilance is no longer necessary. And other persons must respond with concern and respect for the victim's full plight, including his or her efforts toward sensemaking. All three components are essential for recovery of one's prior life as well as for development of a fuller sense of responsibility, reciprocity, and community. But no component is guaranteed. The absence of any of them eventuates in a deepened victimization of isolation, despair, bitterness, and resignation. (Fischer & Wertz, 1979, p. 149)

Composite Structural Description:
Aanstoos's Study of Being Left Out

The second example of a Composite Structural Description is borrowed from Aanstoos's (1987) investigation of the experience of being left out. Here too the account is alive, vivid, and clear in bringing to life the universal character and dynamics of the experience.

Experiencing ourselves as left out evokes an intensely disquieting and painful emotional storm. Previously taken for granted meanings of who we are for others, and who they are for us, are sundered from their past familiar anchors, and now become highly questionable. The smooth reciprocity of self-other relations gives way, and we are confronted by a disturbing negativity. This negativity expresses itself as a tear in the unfolding tapestry of mutual recognition between ourselves and the others. This gap may be a fissure or an abyss, but it discloses an essential break in our connectedness with others.

We become attuned to such a rupture specifically in those situations in which we experience a heightened vulnerability to isolation as a virtual possibility, and, with it, a need for reassurance that we truly matter to the other. Essentially, these are occasions in which there is some sort of social gathering, formal or informal: a coming together that will thematize the bonds between people who care about each other. But our own place within this interpersonal circle is unclear, ambiguous; it requires a clarifying invitation from another. We look, with trepidation, to the other; but our appeal goes unheeded, even unnoticed. Rather than finding the mutuality we sought, we discover instead and in horror that we are invisible to the others, to those who matter to us, and whose solicitude we had wanted so badly. In this way, the previous gnawing possibility of isolation proves inescapable; its preceding virtuality now becomes an all-consuming reality. We find ourselves left out of the circle of reciprocal recognition and acceptance. (Aanstoos, 1987, p. 141)

Textural-Structural Synthesis

The final step of my phenomenological model requires an integration of the composite textural and composite structural descriptions, providing a synthesis of the meanings and essences of the experience.

I have selected three examples: Yoder's (1990) study of guilt, Rhodes's (1987) portrayal of women's movement from dependency to autonomy, and Palaian's (1993) synthesis of the experience of longing.

Synthesis of Guilt: Yoder

Yoder's (1990) analysis of the Composite Textural Description and the Composite Structural Description of her co-researchers' experience of guilt weaves texture and structure together and organizes the qualities and themes into group or universal essences of guilt.

Feelings of guilt are signs of significant turbulence, flaring up within the person. They come like a storm with lightening and cold winds. "It felt like mists, cold wind, dark streets, uncomfortable things. Stormy clouds in the sky. Occasional flashes of lightening. Empty beaches on a cold day. A cold wind from the water."

Guilt feelings close in. They are an imprisonment in which there is no way out. "You feel closed in when you are really feeling guilty. You feel cramped, very claustrophobic, limited, constricted, walled in."

"The feeling of guilt is sharp and jagged. It is "being on the hook," a "knife," a pain as sharp as a surgical incision. The feeling of guilt is fast. "I'm thinking of lightening because it is a jab."

Guilt feelings are "a heavy weight." They are experienced as a "crushing blow." The feeling of guilt pushes, removes, evokes withdrawal, a sinking enormously heavy feeling. It comes in waves. "This intense push that jolts me back." "I'm gonna sink down. It's like this weight is on me."

Feeling guilty is "being in a shell," an invisible agent in a "world of strangers." Guilt feelings send one adrift into space where time is unending and the link with others is severed and closed. There is no hope of repair, renewal, belonging, no chance of even recognizing a genuine self.

The experience of feeling guilty is the experience of being forcibly removed from the flow of everyday life, from the world of ordinary human sharing and warmth. When we feel guilty, we are cast into a painful, frozen, inner-focused world that takes over the self and creates a reality of its own. Guilt feelings sever our sense of connectedness with everyday things, with other people and with ourselves. In the experience of feeling guilty, time stands still. All exits are closed. We are isolated and trapped within ourselves.

In guilt feelings, self-respect deteriorates, a sense of physical ugliness often awakens. Real emotions are hidden. Masked ways of being show themselves in pleasing others. In everyday and in ultimate moments, "The real me is not good enough. Not ever."

Time is experienced as slowed down and unchangeable. Clock time goes haywire. Everything churns and then freezes. Only the crystallized moment of guilt endures. The past is relived over and over again, an endless recycling, a movie that repeats itself without any genuine change or realization.

In guilt feelings, the relationship to the body is also affected. The body becomes distant, moves like a robot. It is in pain, anxious to move somehow, yet, at the same time, fearful that any action will reawaken the scenes of guilt.

In spite of the torturous feelings and helpless, endless, sense of guilt, there is still within the self, the possibility of recovering oneself and regaining the sense of harmonious flow with life. There is the potential to come to terms with the guilt, accept it, share it with another and, in this acceptance, find a way to peace. What is required is the courage to take the first step and risk scornful judgment and the pain of acknowledging one's limitations. There is no guarantee that if one freely and honestly expresses the guilt, and recognizes the vulnerability and limitedness of the self, that the guilty feelings will be excised permanently, but for some of my co-researchers this acceptance and sharing enabled them to reclaim themselves and reestablish inner tranquility. (Yoder, 1990, pp. 111-114) [Reprinted by permission of the author.]

Synthesis of Women's Movement
From Dependency to Autonomy: Rhodes

Rhodes (1987) offers a vivid presentation of textural and structural meanings in her synthesis of Women's Movement From Dependency to Autonomy. She describes the challenges of three major transition points— dependency on the other's priorities, movement toward reconstructing the self and relationship to others, and discovering a new path of self-chosen activities and ways of living and relating. The process of change is highlighted and accentuated in women's stories of the shift from being directed, dominated, and controlled by significant others to exploring and finding directions and ways of being from within oneself.

The movement of women in an intimate relationship from dependency to autonomy is characterized by distinctive qualities in each of three major transition periods. Of particular importance in the dependency phase is the woman's sense of her self. To the degree that it is determined by her mate's priorities (experienced as an inferior part of a larger whole, which would include the culture and the marital system), the woman's identity becomes subservient to that of her husband.

The women in this study started marriage believing that they were expected to take care of the home, the children and their husbands. In turn they would be financially supported and emotionally and sexually rewarded by their mates. Self-esteem would be experienced vicariously through the successes of the husband. The submerging of the self into that of the male and the family was the common adaptation, however varied were the particulars.

In the beginning of the intimate relationship, the women in my study, without exception, were deeply entrenched in patterns of dependency that included transfer of power from parents to mate. The transfer included choices, decision making, preferences, and interpretations of what things are and mean. The first transition occurred with the unravelling of the dependency in the conscious realization of feeling trapped, stifled, constricted and denied as a self—an opening out of dependency in movement toward autonomy. The movement phase is characterized by extending activities outside the home which the woman found relevant to self-interests and desires, the claiming of space and time for personal growth pursuits such as classes and jobs. The final transition involves an entering into the autonomy phase. This transition is marked by a heightening of self-esteem and self-confidence, a determination to be a person with rights, a discovery of the meaning and value of work.

Dependency

In essence, four core themes characterized the dependency phase. Each of these is briefly explicated as follows:

Participants found life confining and predictable, although initially this was viewed as a pleasure. They had fun "playing house" in a life pervaded by a sense of security and safety. Slipping into their dream role with a mate they had gotten what they were socialized to need and want.

The study participants dreamed of being the perfect wife and mother. The desire to fulfill the dream and be taken care of would be provided for by union with a male. Like empty vessels waiting to be filled, the women experienced no authentic sense of "self." By their unwitting bow to cultural programming, women set themselves up for subservience and the impossible dream of the perfect wife and mother.

2. *Blurring of the Self:* The dependency phase was replete with shyness, self-consciousness, a sense of inferiority and helplessness. Fear of exposure to judgments of imperfection as wife, homemaker and/or mother and a general low self-esteem kept these women home, away from the eyes of a judgmental world. Paradoxically, although there was only a vague sense of self, critical self-consciousness was the women's constant companion. Monitored by themselves, as well as others, my participants rarely experienced a sense of freedom or spontaneity, either verbally or physically. Blocked and pressed back into themselves, they had only limited options for personal growth. They were frequently frustrated and angry—with themselves and with life.

The subsumed self provided a protective mist between their own eyes and those of the world. Afraid of speaking out or going after what they wanted, they believed somehow that they would fulfill the ideals of wife and motherhood.

They were not to think for themselves, so thinking had the quality of an echo chamber, ideas reverberated and went nowhere or came rattling back to them, limp and dull, with only a hint of the pain of being minimized and denied by a patriarchal marriage and world.

3. *Surrender of Personal and Economic Power:* My co-researchers characteristically mortgaged their self development for a share of their dream. Marriage brought them a semblance of wish gratification and self-esteem as they proved that they could get their man and achieve what they were expected to achieve, but the abandonment of their own career and economic resources cost them a sense of genuine self-esteem.

Although stepping into the dream was achieved by attaching themselves to a male, the surrender of personal and economic power closed options; space in life became constricted and narrow. Surrendering personal and economic power forced my participants into a position of wheedling for money and consciously being manipulative while experiencing feelings of alienation and powerlessness.

4. *The Sexual Object: No Connection Between Sex and the Self.* In 1984, a syndicated advice columnist, in reporting that about seventy percent of the approximately eighty thousand women who responded to her question about intercourse, indicated that the women would rather do without sex, that hugging and other forms of affection would do. While this was not a scientifically valid sampling, the view of the women surveyed was similar to the position of my co-researchers. My participants during the dependency phase were dissatisfied with their body appearance. They were inexperienced and self-conscious. Sex was at first frightening and eventually came to be

dreaded, as women typically were pushed into participation. Sex was either a problem or made one at the sexual whims of the husband. They generally preferred to avoid sex and some experienced any form of tactile stimulation, including kissing, as disgusting.

Rather than experiencing themselves as mutual sexual participants, the women in my study felt invaded and cheated, and often became "frigid." Almost daily, these women thought about how they would deal with sex, not from the standpoint of their own desires or pleasures, but rather, in imagining tactics for avoiding the sexual encounter. Yet they felt troubled knowing that conflict would ensue should they deprive their men of the sexual forays and release.

Restricted by children, husband, financial dependency and lack of training, and hampered by feelings of inadequacy, the essence of the women's experience was an inability to move or change. Allowing life to be controlled and directed by others, feeling inferior, helpless, confused, and fearful of change, my co-researchers, like zombies, were engulfed in the stifling, suspended grip of immobilization. Like prisoners, they had little power over the content or direction of their lives.

Movement

The women in my study began to wade through fear and depression. Hungering for something different in life, looking for something without knowing what they fell into a depression. Some came to a virtual standstill; others struggled until the weight of inertia and the pain were intolerable. Ultimately, for all of my participants, movement began. Dependency was no longer the desired path.

The essence of movement is the search for self and re-orientationship in an intimate relationship. The relationship change required either physical separation or re-establishment of the known relationship on a different level. The search and change process involved testing as well as feeling fearful, brave, muddled, befuddled, confused, and conflicted in relationships that were both tightening and loosening. New roles were hard to come by, still, women in this study struggled forward, working against social constraints and against those constraints that lived inside.

According to my participants, the bind of women's cultural role began to loosen with the Women's Movement, which explored and clarified women's lives. Up to this point in time, not daring to let themselves recognize what they already knew, they found this information enlightening. It encouraged freedom and experimentation. Since we can only know those things that exist in our consciousness and make choices from those alternatives, my participants were powerfully affected by the philosophy of the movement. All the co-researchers indicated that they were touched positively by the Women's Movement. It gave them concrete ideas about how they had been living and offered alternatives.

My participants began searching, trying to find what was inside, catching a glimpse of the depth within, grasping at that elusive self, at the possibilities for life, based on self-interest, desire, and choice. The themes presented below were key dimensions of movement for each

1. *Surfacing of the Self:* The intertwining, narrow, confining experience of "self" as a personification of the feminine role model began to change as participants allowed their thinking to surface, to be explored and to guide awareness and choice. At first, they denied thoughts and feelings which were outside the role, viewing them as a threat to life as it was known, regardless of uneasiness or discomfort or unhappiness, depression, or pain. It was easier to listen to past voices and to remain in the wife-mother role than to press for a different future.

As these feelings shifted, the women began to reach out to others and to an individual life outside the home. Immediately, they recognized that change was necessary and that options were available. A fundamental search was activated for a self recognized as legitimate, a search for women's own preference and enjoyment. An expanded life was now the goal of my participants.

The hunger for something different for the self and in relationships was profound. The mysterious promise in life was almost tangible. Conflicted, wanting something, unable to say clearly what it was, but knowing the imperative need to change, women vacillated from feeling strong to feeling week, from feeling confident to feeling confused and fearful.

2. *Separation from the Dependency:* Separating from the symbiotic tie to a mate, my participants took their first step toward independence. Husbands were viewed as consciously or unconsciously inhibiting the strivings for an authentic "self." . . . In every case, the women felt restricted and struggled to discover their own freedom and power. For some participants, heated arguments and debates were daily fare. Confronting the partner, they stepped forward with heightened determination to find what they wanted and needed for themselves. Viewed in retrospect, relationship alterations occurred like time studies in slow motion. Changes that appeared impulsive had taken years to materialize.

For women in the study, separation was the essential ingredient in finding the "self" and becoming autonomous. The primary challenge in the search for the "self" became the struggle to be separate. A separate person was the essential action in prying open a false identity.

3. *Movement Activities:* Turning within, exploring and seeking answers, women in the study began the change process, setting out to test themselves. In their search within, women found the confidence and strength to start school, return to school, or get a job. Rather then following their old

reactive style, they took action. In three cases, death of the spouse provided the action impetus. A decision had to be made regarding the family business and these three women took over.

By experimenting with decision-making and being definitive with plans for themselves, participants slowly began to trust themselves. They burst out of dependency restrictions and took control of a part of life by making decisions and following through. There were some false starts, such as taking a class and then dropping it, applying for jobs and not following through or starting a job and quitting. These experiences, however, seemed to be helpful as women tentatively stretched, a little bit ahead of themselves, then pulled back, satisfied they had tried, and dissatisfied with not following through. Temporary setbacks strengthened the desire not to disappoint themselves again.

Activities outside the home helped participants feel more alive, but for some women the foot out the door was in danger. One participant was so frightened by the possibility of finishing school and the performance anxiety of being prepared to enter the world that she plucked the safety of ill health around her and temporarily closed down.

The movement away from living dependently was typically approached timidly. Gradually self-imposed restrictions were unblocked and the search for "self opened new possibilities and directions."

Autonomy

Either as students or in jobs, participants looked for meaningful directions. They were seldom clear about what jobs would enhance them or where to find them. However, once a career was zeroed in on, participants put everything into it. Responsible and dedicated, finding increasing value in the inner experience of pleasure and mastery, they found relationships dramatically changed. Further, experiencing pleasure in their sense of a being-in-the-world, participants could allow themselves to be authentic and begin to have a full experience of themselves.

Still shaking off the shackles and, at times, caught in the past, the women saw the light of hope and promise brightened this new path as women in the study slowly gained momentum and began embarking on a new experience, living life through the desires and decisions of their own self. The search was successful, the feelings tenuous.

As participants moved toward new ways of being, internal and social constraints gave way very slowly. Never overcoming all barriers, women found that dependency threads continued to be woven into the autonomous life.

My research participants were bewildered at how autonomy occurred, yet somehow they broke through into an autonomous life style, looked around, and were surprised like Dorothy, finding the Wizard of Oz. The mental blur, the early defensive style of coming at life from around the corner, never confronting issues, sometimes returned. The shock of an independent life at first frightened them. They felt confused, rocky but very happy; they were autonomous physically but the "spirit hadn't kicked in yet." Feeling increasingly free, and in command of "self," my participants in time experienced a sense of competence and self-confidence in ever expanding spaces. (Rhodes, 1987, pp. 119-128) [Reprinted by permission of author]

Synthesis of Longing: Palaian

From her composite textural and composite structural "experience of longing," Palaian (1993) developed a unity of texture and structure in her synthesis of qualities, meanings and essences of "longing." Longing is no longer disguised and hidden but comes to clear elucidations in Palaian's portrayal of the experience.

The experience of longing is a paradoxical experience leaving the experiencer in a dilemma, a double-bind, a Catch-22. Longing turns in on itself. One reaches out across an expanse toward fulfillment in trust and hope. In the reaching out pain and loss are experienced and an imminent yearning for fulfillment.

Longing is the grief of the unattainable, the impossible. It is the hope toward possibility and infinite entrancement. Both despair and promise exist together in longing, rhythms of death and birth, birth and death. There is movement forward across expanses so wide one cannot see the other side and must trust and rationalize that, "There is something to move toward." Yet the motion is also backward, recoiling one which nurses the wounds of separation and aloneness.

Nothing is there, yet there is something felt, a presence the experiencers of longing cannot remember. They reach out deliberately and with intent toward the hope for release of pain. They elicit the pain, the frustration, the anguish living within. Longing is at the interface of the losses of yesterday, the open wounds of separation, and the joyful creations of tomorrow.

Longing hurts so desperately and still it continues; still the hunger, and the itch arises within. It is the primitive pulse of life, a primordial memory of who one has been. It calls the experiencers, drawing them nearer toward meaning, toward fulfillment, toward connection, toward the self.

Longing reaches for freedom, for space, for time, for self. There is rhythm; there is an intricate balance between satisfaction and the insatiable quest for more. The seed has been planted, the promise made, the pilgrimage set out upon.

Experiencers must traverse the land, seeking the bridge between who they have been and who they can be. They travail across the disparity, the discord of who they are and who they imagine they can be. This longing movement forges the infiniteness of inner imaginings and enriches the connections here on earth.

Longing is a complete and utter mystery to its experiencers. It is suffering and it is pleasure. It is inside yet it is outside. It is permanent and ever-present, yet it changes so quickly, often and in many ways.

Longing is tricky, elusive, quick as a frightened deer running through the forest. One is left unsure if it will ever leave and also left hoping for its return.

The experience of longing is a thirst to connect deeply. The myriad objects of connection are unique expressions of humanity. Like fingerprints, they reveal whole worlds of each person's inner self. They reveal individual constellations of desire and unique journeys of possibility, wholeness, completion, love.

The longing moves so silently, and so quickly is in search of itself, freely romping and gallantly jumping. Longing is the fuel which keeps the inner fires aflame. It evokes passions which burn brightly, eternally, always calling.

Longing is an act of redemption. It aims ultimately to make life good again, to bring forth meaning again, to evoke life again. It is the pale translucent green bud emerging from a desolate burnt out ground. It is the seedling which sprouts from the emptiness, after the destruction.

Longing is life calling itself to itself. It is symbolized by the streams and tributaries of lakes and oceans and waters that flourish within. It is also a thundering storm, or a misty morning dew, waters absorbed by gentle capillaries.

The longing experience is regenerative. It guides, persuades, and coaxes the person toward connectedness, toward what one hungers for, the call of being and of loving kindness. Longing entices, encourages, creates forward movement. Longing is new life, connected to life, to the pulse of life.

The experience of longing points to the invisible, unnameable mystery which is in the world and yet beyond it. Longing is rooted in the here and now intensely yet just as clearly it is a yearning for the eternal, the pure and perfect belonging to self and other. (Palaian, 1993, pp. 92-95) [Reprinted by permission of the author]

In closing this chapter on applications of transcendental phenomenological research, I refer the reader to Appendix C, which presents a detailed outline summary of the transcendental phenomenological model (Epoche,

Phenomenological Reduction, Imaginative Variation, and Synthesis of Texture and Structure) and methods and procedures for preparing to collect, collecting, and analyzing data as well as implications and outcomes that may be considered in summing up a transcendental phenomenological research project.

REFERENCES

Aanstoos, C. M. (1987). A descriptive phenomenology of the experience of being left out. In F. J. van Zuuren, F. J. Wertz, & B. Mook (Eds.), *Advances in qualitative psychology: Themes and variations* (pp. 137-155). Berwyn, PA: Swets North America.

Buckley, F. M. (1971). An approach to a phenomenology of at-homeness. In A. Giorgi, W. F. Fischer, & R. Von Eckartsberg (Eds.), *Duquesne studies in phenomenological psychology* (Vol. 1, pp. 198-211). Pittsburgh: Duquesne University Press.

Colaizzi, P. R. (1973). *Reflection and research in psychology.* Dubuque, IA: Kendall/Hunt.

Copen, R. (1993). Insomnia: A phenomenological investigation. (Doctoral dissertation, The Union Institute, 1992). *Dissertation Abstracts International, 53,* 6542B.

de Koning, A. J. J. (1979). The qualitative method of research in the phenomenology of suspicion. In A. Giorgi, R. Knowles, & D. L. Smith (Eds.), *Duquesne studies in phenomenological psychology* (Vol. 3, pp. 122-134). Pittsburgh: Duquesne University Press.

Fischer, C. T., & Wertz, F. J. (1979). Empirical phenomenological analyses of being criminally victimized. In A. Giorgi, R. Knowles, & D. L. Smith (Eds.), *Duquesne studies in phenomenological psychology* (Vol. 3, pp. 135-158). Pittsburgh: Duquesne University Press.

Fraelich, C. B. (1989). A phenomenological investigation of the psychotherapist's experience of presence. (Doctoral dissertation, The Union Institute, 1988). *Dissertation Abstracts International, 50,* 1643B.

Humphrey, E. (1991). Searching for life's meaning: A phenomenological and heuristic exploration of the experience of searching for meaning in life. (Doctoral dissertation, The Union Institute, 1992). *Dissertation Abstracts International, 51,* 4051B.

Keen, E. (1975). *Doing research phenomenologically.* Unpublished manuscript, Bucknell University, Lewisburg, PA.

Miesel, J. A. (1991). A phenomenological exploration of the experience of voluntarily changing one's career during midlife. (Doctoral dissertation, The Union Institute, 1991). *Dissertation Abstracts International, 52,* 5542B.

Palaian, S. (1993). The experience of longing: A phenomenological investigation. (Doctoral dissertation, The Union Institute, 1993). *Dissertation Abstracts International, 54,* 1678B.

Palmieri, C. (1990). The experience of adults abused as children. (Doctoral dissertation, The Union Institute, 1990). *Dissertation Abstracts International, 51,* 2631B.

Rhodes, C. (1987). Women in transition: From dependency to autonomy A study in self development. (Doctoral dissertation, The Union Graduate School, 1986). *Dissertation Abstracts International, 48,* 572B.

Stevick, E. L. (1971). An empirical investigation of the experience of anger. In A. Giorgi, W. Fisher, & R. Von Eckartsberg (Eds.), *Duquesne studies in phenomenological psychology* (Vol. 1, pp. 132-148). Pittsburgh: Duquesne University Press.

Trumbull, M. (1993). The experience of undergoing coronary artery bypass surgery: A phenomenological investigation. (Doctoral dissertation, The Union Institute, 1993). *Dissertation Abstracts International, 54,* 1115B.

van Kaam, A. (1959). Phenomenal analysis: Exemplified by a study of the experience of "really feeling understood." *Journal of Individual Psychology, 15*(1), 66-72.

van Kaam, A. (1966). Application of the phenomenological method. In A. van Kaam, *Existential foundations of psychology.* Lanham, MD: University Press of America.

Yoder, P. (1990). Guilt, the feeling and the force: A phenomenological study of the experience of feeling guilty. (Doctoral dissertation, The Union Institute, 1989). *Dissertation Abstracts International, 50,* 5341B.

8

SUMMARY, IMPLICATIONS, AND OUTCOMES
A Phenomenological Analysis

Following the organization, presentation, and analysis of data derived from a phenomenological investigation, the researcher summarizes the study in its entirety and considers possible limitations. The researcher returns to the literature review and distinguishes her or his findings from prior research, outlines a future research project that would advance knowledge on the topic, and discusses the outcomes of the investigation in terms of social meanings and implications as well as personal and professional values. Each of these ending phases of a phenomenological investigation is illustrated from various phenomenological research projects for which I served as faculty advisor and reviewer. As a closing of the chapter, I include a complete outline for developing a phenomenological research manuscript.

SUMMARY OF ENTIRE STUDY

Schmidt's Investigation of the Shadow Archetype

Schmidt (1992) studied how people perceive and describe their experience of the Jungian shadow archetype. From lengthy interviews with co-researchers he was able to determine the qualities, themes, meanings, and essences of the shadow experience. I have selected Schmidt's presentation as a good example of the researcher's development of a summary of an entire research project. In the summary, Schmidt describes the personal and professional factors that motivated him to investigate the shadow archetype. He briefly points to prior research most directly related to his study. He outlines the transcendental phenomenological design and methodology that guided his investigation, presents his research findings, and discusses implications and outcomes emerging from his analysis of the data.

Development of a summary section of transcendental phenomenological research is an important challenge. It offers a kind of abstract of an entire investigation and in a brief span of material enables other researchers to determine its relevance to their own research pursuits and whether or not to review the entire research report.

With minor modifications, the following is a verbatim account of Schmidt's summary of his research.

In chapter one, I detailed how I became interested in studying the shadow as a Jungian archetype and how Carl Jung, the founder of analytic psychology, heuristically explored the inner domain of his unconscious, namely the shadow archetype. I focused on the heroic undertaking of facing the shadow and how this journey of the self is fraught with peril. I examined the various challenges to my Jewish forebears, who struggled with the collective German shadow of Nazism. Further, I discussed the intertwining of the personal and the collective shadow and how I, as a descendant of German Jews, am also a carrier of the collective Teutonic shadow archetype. This chapter also depicted the various incarnations of my shadow, culminating in the pursuit of my dissertation question: "What is the experience of the shadow as a Jungian archetype?"

In chapter two, I researched Jungian theoretical perspectives of the shadow archetype. I discussed the collective unconscious and the role it plays in the evolution of the shadow. I also included descriptions of the underlying meanings of archetypes and archetypal images, and the psychological developmental stages theorized about the shadow itself. I focused on the primary method, psychological projection, that Jung believed propels the shadow into consciousness.

In chapter three, I carefully reviewed the relevant literature on the shadow archetype. I concentrated on research studies of the shadow. Since I found a scarcity of these kinds of investigations, I also reviewed conceptual and applied journal articles. I noted the commonality of definition of the shadow in each of the research dissertations that I studied and a strict adherence to other Jungian theories related to the shadow. I also discussed how the research literature goes to great lengths to conclude that Jungian theories on the shadow and the other archetypes are not mere copies of Freud's earlier expositions on the unconscious. Jungian studies referred to the shadow as a catalyst for individuation and self-actualization as well as a doorway to the deeper inclines of the personal and collective unconscious. Reference was also made to the friction created between some of the Eastern philosophical ideas underlying the shadow and those of the West. The various layers of structure of the shadow were reviewed, including the personal, collective, and archetypal. Finally, good and evil and their roles in terms of the shadow archetype were elucidated.

Chapter four is an examination of the phenomenological research approach that I employed. I reviewed the history of phenomenology and key concepts of its founder, Edmund Husserl. These concepts included consciousness as a form of being, the return to "things" themselves, and a strategic retreat from all forms of philosophical dualism. I chose four key research concepts to focus on: namely, life-world, structure-texture, intentionality, and the phenomenological methods of description. I then explored how these concepts impacted my study of the shadow archetype.

Chapter five elucidated the structures and textures of my research findings. I discovered that the shadow has one universal structure: the self related to self-experience. This was followed by several substructures, including existential ambiguity, self-fulfilling prophecies, portals to personal growth, the dark twin as a subpersonality, polar opposites, and narcissism.

The core thematic textures of the shadow that were uncovered included: the shadow as embodied in the experiences of preconscious demonic entities; a personal evil; the shadow as released through intense negative emotions and inner turmoil; and the shadow as embodied in individual ambiguity: a pervasive mental consternation.

In the final chapter of my dissertation, I will summarize what I have discovered about the experience of the shadow archetype and its relevance to me, to the field of psychology, and to other areas of study including international relations and anthropology. I will also critique my research methods and procedures, including the limits and advantages of my research design and methodology, as well as what I would do differently in future studies of this nature. I will distinguish the findings of my research investigation from those summarized in my literature review. I will close with a discussion of the variance between the shadow archetypal experience and that of the direct experiencing of evil. (Schmidt, 1992, pp. 141-144)

In each of the next sections, a major component of the *summary* section of a research project is presented in detail. Each section provides critical material useful in assessing verification and plausibility of the methodology, the data, and implications of the study.

Trumbull's Investigation of Coronary Artery Bypass Surgery

Distinguishing Findings From Prior Research

In Trumbull's (1993) study of coronary artery bypass surgery, he conducted comprehensive interviews with 14 co-researchers. He analyzed the verbatim interviews and developed individual and composite textural and structural descriptions, as well as a synthesis of meanings and essences. In the following excerpt he distinguishes his findings from prior research and points to the original knowledge derived from his analysis of the nature and essence of coronary artery bypass surgery as described in first-person accounts of research participants who were willing to offer comprehensive portrayals of their experience.

Having collected and analyzed my data, I will now position my study and its findings in relation to my review of the literature. In Chapter Three, Literature Review: On Coronary Artery Bypass Surgery, I reviewed one hundred and fifty-two citations and categorized them into nine areas: 1) pre- and post-psychosocial impact, outcomes, and quality of life as a result of CABG, 2) Educational informational materials for individuals who have had or will have CABG, 3) Autobiographical accounts of health care providers and laypersons on the experience of CABG, 4) Impact of CABG on spouse/family, 5) Case studies of specific psychiatric disorders and the effects of CABG, 6) Medications and their impact on pre- and post-CABG, 7) How to prevent further problems through diet and lifestyle changes for individuals who have had a CABG, 8) Medication vs CABG, 9) A qualitative study of the CABG experience, using content analysis. I will comment on the similarities and differences between my study and each of the above categories under separate subheadings.

Pre- and Post-Psychosocial Impact, Outcomes, and Quality of Life as a Result of CABG

In the first category, Pre- and post psychological impact, outcomes and quality of life, the foci of the majority of these studies diverged from my own. They measured depression and other psychological states pre- and post-surgically. They also measured Type A behavior versus Type B behavior, the impact of hypnosis on CABG outcomes, psychiatric outcomes of men versus women, preoperative preparation to reduce incidence of acute postoperative hypertension, gender differences in compliance behavior. My study did not seek to measure any of these variables.

Comparing and Distinguishing Findings
of My Research With Prior Studies

Four of the studies in this category, presented below, were similar to outcomes of my research.

Mulgan and Logan (1990) completed a study on the psychosocial effects for patients and spouses as they waited for CABG. They found increased spousal anxiety; 45 percent of the patients claimed their health had suffered. The researchers recommended that more attention be given to both patients and spouses during the waiting period. My co-researchers reported the same concerns and offered the same suggestions.

Saudia, Kinney, Brown, and Young-Ward (1991) conducted a study examining the relationship between health locus of control and helpfulness of prayer as a coping mechanism prior to surgery. They found no correlation between the styles of health locus of control and helpfulness of prayer. However, they did find that whatever style was employed, the patient perceived prayer to be beneficial. The researchers' findings were consistent with my own. All of my co-researchers, but one, reported that they had examined their religious beliefs and were putting their lives in God's hands.

Penckofer and Holm (1987) studied the hopes and fears that stood out after CABG. Consistent with my study, they found that as more time passed after the surgery, the individual expressed more hope than fear and was optimistic about the future relevant to improved health, good family life, and physical activity. Fears of patients of persistent incisional pain, return of angina, and another round of bypass surgery were also described by my co-researchers.

My data were similar to the data collected by Thurer, Levine and Thurer (1980) in the following areas: Both before and after surgery, many patients reacted with: a) Denial, b) Mourning, and c) Revering of their surgeon. Following the surgery, the patients: a) Reviewed what was important in life and changed priorities (valuing human closeness and devaluing work), b) Recognized their mortality and developed a renewed interest in life.

Educational/Informational Materials for
Individuals Who Have Had or Will Have CABG

I found thirteen publications that presented educational/informational materials for individuals who have had or were planning to have CABG. Three of these were studies; the remainder were books, guides, pamphlets, and a video. The three studies confirmed my finding that the time the medical staff took to prepare, inform, and educate the patient was critical in helping the patient cope with the procedures and interventions that they had to face. Cupples (1991) reported that individuals who received pre-admission, post-admission, and preoperative education developed a significantly higher preoperative knowledge, more positive mood states, and more favorable physiological recovery. My study confirmed these findings.

Also consistent with my findings was the study completed by Dracup, Moser, Marseden, Taylor and Guzy (1991). These researchers investigated the effects of a multidimensional cardiopulmonary rehabilitation program on psychosocial functioning and reported that those who participated in the rehabilitation program were significantly less anxious and depressed, were more satisfied with their marriages, and had made a better overall psychosocial adjustment.

Beckie (1989) studied the effects of a supportive/educative telephone program for six weeks after leaving the hospital. She found that the individuals who had more knowledge about coronary artery disease, diet, medication, physical activity and its restrictions, as well as participating in rhythms of exercise and rest, experienced lower levels of anxiety. These findings were also consistent with my study.

Autobiographical Accounts of Health Care Providers and a Layperson on the Experience of CABG

The third category of my prior research analysis included thirteen investigations. All thirteen noted eight themes and were the same as those in my own study. However, none included a reflective analysis of data, which was a highlight of my study.

Impact of CABG on Spouse and Family

The impact of CABG on spouse and family, the fourth category of my review of research, included nine investigations. My research replicated the findings of these studies, emphasizing the critical importance of support and care by family and friends in helping the patient cope with the crisis of CABG. Four of these studies: Radley, Green (1986); Goldschmidt, Brooks, Sethia, Wheatley, and Bond (1984); Gilliss (1984); and Langeluddecke, Tennant, Fulcher, Bariad, and Hughes (1989) reported clinically significant symptoms of anxiety, depression, and global psychosocial impairment of spouses preoperatively and subsequent improvement post-surgically. All of the researchers recommended that nurses be responsive to the needs of family and friends, and that specific programs be developed to help spouse and family members cope with the stress of the surgery and its aftermath. In addition, my co-researchers described the negative impact of surgery on spouse and family and suggested that the issues be addressed prior to surgery.

Case Studies of Specific Psychiatric Disorders and the Effects of CABG, and Medications and Its Impact Pre- and Post-CABG

Category Five of my literature review, Case Studies involving specific psychiatric disorders and the effects of CABG, and Category Six, Medication and its impact pre- and post-CABG were examined as illustrations of the breadth of the literature. My own study explored a completely different question the purpose of which was to search into the nature, meanings and essences of CABG.

How to Prevent Further Problems Through Diet and Lifestyle Changes for Individuals Who Have Had a CABG

Category Seven of the literature review, "How to prevent further problems through diet and lifestyle changes for individuals who have had a CABG" involved three investigations. All of my co-researchers were highly motivated to make dietary and lifestyle changes in order to improve their health. They utilized rehabilitation and exercise programs, took dietary and cooking classes, purchased relevant books, and were consistent and persistent in making appropriate changes. Thus, my findings pointed to similar lifestyle changes but they were described from the vantage point of the first-person accounts of my co-researchers.

Medications vs CABG

Category Eight, Medications vs CABG, was also included to illustrate the breadth of the literature. My own research focused on a different topic and thus was not concerned with this issue.

A Qualitative Study of the CABG Experience, Using Content Analysis

The final Category, Nine, involved a qualitative study of the CABG experience, using content analysis. Bartz (1988) reported findings related to transitions from dependence to independence. It included five phases: 1) Surviving the surgery, 2) Coming to awareness, 3) Sensing physical injury, 4) Sensing the surroundings, and 5) Interpersonal confidence in their physician. These findings were replicated in my own study, however, Bartz did not provide individual and composite textural or structural depictions, or a synthesis presenting the whole of the experience of undergoing coronary artery bypass surgery.

In positioning my study within the context of prior research and reports I have shown where my research replicated the findings of earlier studies. I have also pointed out the differences. From my study, I derived eight core themes and unified them into a composite textural description of the experience of undergoing coronary artery bypass surgery. Using imaginative variation, I developed a composite structural description of the experience. I integrated the composite textural and structural descriptions into a synthesis of meanings and essences of the experience of undergoing coronary artery bypass surgery. (Trumbull, 1993, pp. 211-219) [Reprinted by permission of the author]

FUTURE STUDIES

In a phenomenological investigation the researcher, during the course of the study, becomes an expert on the topic, knows the nature and findings of prior research, has developed new knowledge on the topic, and has become proficient in recognizing the kinds of future research that would deepen and extend knowledge on the topic.

I have selected two investigations to illustrate how a researcher might approach a discussion of and outline for future research: Alpern's (1984) investigation of "Men's Experience of Menstruation" and Paskiewicz's (1988) study of the "Traumatic Closed Head Injury."

Alpern's Investigation of Men's Experience of Menstruation

Alpern (1984) interviewed a carefully selected group of men in lengthy individual sessions as a way of obtaining information on how they perceived and described their experience of menstruation. She offers important suggestions for future research projects and briefly points to ways of designing them. For example, future research might include group rather than individual interviews of men's experience of menstruation. Another approach that Alpern suggests as a future possibility involves the interviewing of male-female couples to compare and contrast their experience.

The following excerpt from her investigation of men's experience of menstruation outlines Alpern's views on what she regards as significant new directions for understanding the experience of menstruation.

In this study, data was obtained during individual interviews and experience of viewing a film on menstruation. Varying the form and considering the findings offer additional insights into men's experience of menstruation.

An outstanding feature of the design of this study was that I, the researcher, am a woman. While this is not necessarily a limitation and, in fact, one co-researcher regarded it as an asset, it did influence the men's perceptions. A study in which a man conducted interviews on this topic might yield different or additional data.

By design, the men in the study did not interact with one another. The lack of verbal contact was pointed out by several men. Universally, the men expressed a curiosity about other men's feelings and attitudes about menstruation. A study that included group interaction might evoke reactions and aspects of men's experiences that were not tapped by the privacy of individual interviews. Group dialogue could include all men, as well as women and men together.

Interviewing couples, a man and a woman, who are intimately involved, would provide information about perceptions and responses within the context of meaningful relationships. Other relationships that might prove fruitful if examined are parent, mother or father, and child, and doctor and patient.

What was critical to the execution and the outcome of this study was the emphasis on the subjective perspective. The recommendations for further research do not alter this fundamental focus. They propose modifications of the particular subjective perspective or the context in which the data is obtained. Because a major finding of this study is that men's views of menstruation are intimately and integrally related to their being, a repetition of this format or a similar one, might provide additional insights into the personal styles of approaching menstruation. The phenomenological approach offers a description of subjective experience, however, every phenomenon is multi-layered in its make-up and therefore open to continual discovery. This study provided a description of men's experience of menstruation, but not necessarily a complete or total one. Additional investigations of men's experience of menstruation would reveal additional aspects and understandings of the phenomenon. (Alpern, 1984, pp. 150-151)

Paskiewicz's Study of Traumatic Closed Head Injury

Paskiewicz (1988) interviewed 11 co-researchers in studying intensively their experience of suffering and recovering from a traumatic closed head injury. He considered research designs and methods that would deepen and extend the knowledge obtained from his own and prior research on the traumatic closed head injury. He emphasizes that more information is needed on the long-term effect of closed head injuries, thus Paskiewicz proposes a longitudinal study. Dissatisfied with the adequacy of data on the experience of family members, he suggests a future research project in which each family member would be invited to describe in depth the impact of living with a closed head injured person.

In the following verbatim selection, Paskiewicz outlines possible future studies and relates them to his own research design and data.

> Further phenomenological research is needed in the area of head injuries. Two research areas arose in the course of my study that I believe are of particular significance in understanding this phenomenon. The first involves the long term study of head injuries; the second focuses on the experience of family members in living with the head injured person.
>
> Dimken [*sic*] and Reitan (1977) have suggested a need for varied approaches in researching issues related to neurology. One such approach which has received little attention to date is the use of longitudinal studies.
>
> In my own research, I was fortunate in including two individuals who are ten years post-injury. Both of these individuals shared the same essential experience as those persons injured more recently. In terms of rehabilitation both individuals made good to excellent progress, reaching milestones of rehabilitative success. However, their progress seemed to reach a plateau and then declined. Is this the norm? Are there long-term elements in the experience of head injuries that precipitate such a decline? Are there long-term implications for how effectively the individual can cope with the intensity of his or her struggles before "burning out?" Are there interventional strategies at critical points that may move the head injured person forward towards a continuation of the growth process? A phenomenological research design employing interviews of co-researchers whose injuries are over ten years old, aimed at understanding the nature of their experience from their current perspective would address the broad questions outlined above. Improved knowledge of the recovery and decline process would lead the way to creative intervention strategies.
>
> Key to the experience of the head injured person is his or her relationship with others. For this reason, as well as for gaining an understanding of what

the experience is like, a study focusing on the experience of family members would add an important understanding and perhaps point to ways of facilitating and maintaining positive communication between family members and the head injured person. A more complete understanding of the impact on the family is also needed if effective treatment is to be employed. How is it to live in a family with an individual who no longer believes in herself or himself, who feels less worthwhile, to live with the whirlwind of feelings, and be affected by the hiding and withdrawal characterizing the injured person? In what ways does a brain-injured person learn to adapt in the family? What are the factors that lead to the high divorce rate? Two complimentary phenomenological studies are suggested. In the first, adults, spouses or significant others who live with the head injured person in a nuclear social unit both prior to and after the injury, would be interviewed in order to arrive at an understanding of the essence of their experience of living with a person who has been suffering from a head injury. In the second study, adolescent children of head injured adults, who have the perspective of knowing the affected parent at least nine years pre-injury, would be interviewed to gain insight into their experience of living in such a family. The focus would be on how the head injury impacts them as they relate to themselves, individual family members, the family unit as a whole, and those outside the family.

The combination of my own research with the three proposed studies would offer a broad phenomenological perspective of the experience of a head injury from the point of view of those most directly impacted by it. (Paskiewicz, 1988, pp. 103-105) [Reprinted by permission of the author]

OUTCOMES IN TERMS OF SOCIAL
AND PROFESSIONAL IMPLICATIONS

To illustrate the implications of data derived from the investigation, I have selected verbatim material from three studies: Stratman's (1989) "Personal Power for Women," Paskiewicz's (1988) "Traumatic Close Head Injury," and Schneider's (1987) "Mother-Daughter Relationship."

Stratman's Study on Personal Power—Women

Stratman (1990), in lengthy interviews, explored with women their feelings, thoughts, perceptions, and experiences in their quest for personal power. Her data are of particular value in inspiring women to take charge of their lives and affirm their own personal power in making

decisions and responding to challenges. I have selected this section of
Stratman's work as an example of timely, socially relevant research
responding to a long neglected social value.
In the following excerpt from her research project, she discusses the
implications of her findings.

... in the area of human development, personal power has both individual
and societal implications. Personal power colors all life experience. It
enables one to initiate and implement change and to take charge of one's
own life. The present research has similar implications for therapists,
educators, and parents. The ability to internalize affirmation and to become
self affirming is the cornerstone of personal power. With personal power
one is able to make life choices. In exercising personal power and making
life choices, self affirmation is enhanced and personal power is strengthened. Facilitating personal power becomes the task of therapists, educators,
and parents. More specifically, co-researchers described meeting challenges, but not impossible challenges, as facilitating the growth of their
power. Realistic challenges that could be met with success so that the
individual feels powerful were frequently cited. Support of others in early
childhood was an important factor in the early development of personal
power. Co-researchers who recognized inner power as children were told
by important others that they were capable and could do whatever they
chose to do. Women who first recognized power as adults described more
of a struggle for this recognition and a continued need for support from
outside of themselves to experience personal power. It may be that this
affirmation of another is the precursor for actualizing personal power.
These data support the importance of developing self trust in childhood so
that the individual is able to experience his or her power, make his or her
own choices, risk making mistakes, and live more fully. Identifying challenges that are possible, to minimize failure and maximize the probability
of success, is an important task of parents, educators, and therapists. In
therapy, this translates to the therapist's offering both support and challenge. The value of the basic belief that the individual is capable, can take
charge of his or his life, is underlined.
    ... in studying personal power for women, this research provides a
constructive model and support for women who aspire to recognize, utilize,
and befriend their personal power. These depictions of power offer
encouragement to try new behaviors, to learn from the past, and to venture
courageously into an insecure future. There is a valuing of the nurturing,
caring qualities of power which is congruent for women. It is a portrait of
power as feminine . . . as belonging and not alien to women. . . .
    . . . personal power is a human quality which is not externally created
or caused. Personal power can be nourished from without but it is primarily

an inner or self affirmation. For this reason, one individual cannot empower another. The belief that one individual can empower another actually denies the power of that other. One can be respectful and sensitive to the power of another and facilitate optimum conditions for experiencing personal power. In fact, it is our moral responsibility to work toward creating an environment which facilitates personal power; an environment which encourages the synthesis of opposites, responsible decision-making, taking charge of one's life; and an environment which respects and values personal power. It is, however, the responsibility and the necessity of each individual to actualize her personal power.

Finally, implied by all, and clearly stated by some of the co-researchers, is a more mature, responsible experiencing of power that is guided by an awareness of the connection of each individual with others. . . . The socialization experience of women teaches us to become expert in being relational, supportive, and cooperative. These talents, in combination with the more instrumental qualities such as competency, independence, and decision-making, are needed for individual worth, for effective family and social interactions, and even for global coexistence. Inclusion of responsible personal power in leadership roles will benefit both the individual and society.

It seems fitting to close with one co-researcher's experience which provides an eloquent summary of personal power. She states, "Personal power is a flame within me that I have to follow to be me. It looks like a tiny flame that could be easily blown out but really it's one of those perpetual lights. I can go off and leave it or give some of it to others and feel confident that it won't go out. In fact, the more I give my flame to others, the brighter my flame gets, until I don't have to worry about its going out at all. It comes from inside of me but it's brightened by others so that I can proudly say, 'look, this is my flame' and I can follow it. All of my important life decisions are made by the light of this flame. It's the light of integrity, of being true to myself. It becomes my life truth but also the truth of life." Understanding and nourishing the essence of this flame, this truth, this personal power results in individual, as well as societal, growth towards becoming all that one can be. (Stratman, 1990, pp. 162-167) [Reprinted by permission of the author.]

Paskiewicz's Study on Closed Head Injuries

Paskiewicz (1988), having distinguished his findings from prior research, in the following excerpt considers the implications for improving care of persons who have suffered and are recovering from a traumatic closed head injury. Paskiewicz's implications relevant to society's treatment and neglect of closed head injured persons, as well as his suggestions for rehabilitation, offer important directions and resources that would positively impact learning and recovery of competencies of closed head injured persons.

In the following section of his research, Paskiewicz discusses the social and personal implications of his data relevant to improved care of closed head injured persons.

Implications for Improved Care

It is apparent that a head injury has a profound effect on the life of the injured person and on his or her relationships with others. The results of the injury are far reaching and chronic. Prevention, of course, is the primary challenge, requiring much more social concern and attention. The majority of these injuries occur in cars. Programs aimed at responsible driving, the use of seat belts, and new and improved car safety features, such as the addition of air bags in cars, need to be supported.

More suitable and effective means of rehabilitation need to be developed and employed. Many of the participants of this study were placed with developmentally or emotionally impaired people, or left to their own ingenuity and resources to recover. Programming that was available tended to be neglectful of specific issues that the head injured adult faces, especially to consider memory difficulties, energy levels and emotional sensitivity in daily plans and activities. Emotional support and psychotherapeutic opportunities are largely unavailable or rejected. Family issues are not a priority. Ben-Yishay and Diller (1983) [sic] have pointed to three main barriers to recovery: problems of attention, learning, and integration. While unquestionably important in every day [sic] care of closed head injury, a positive attention to these problems would still not deal with the emotional and social aspects of the head injured person's experience.

The need for comprehensive, multi-focused, interdisciplinary treatment is evident. Programs should include: assessment, cognitive retraining, personal counseling, group counseling, family therapy, community activity functions, ongoing medical treatment, and work placement. Research by Diller and Gordon (1981) points to the need for rehabilitation treatment that builds upon medical and psychological diagnosis, refining it and integrating it with the natural healing process.

As evidenced in this study, the emotional component of a head injury is strong and dominant, leading to shattered confidence, withdrawal, and feelings of being alienated and disconnected. Relationships with others are seriously impaired and the ability to relate on an intimate level with family members is blocked. Individual psychotherapy can be useful in alleviating emotional and behavioral distress and in preventing further emotional complications.

The issues encountered in treatment are similar to those seen in a general outpatient population. Persons with a head injury may have different content issues but many of their struggles are the same. This is due to the intense stress that a head injury imposes. An individual will manifest this stress at the "faulty lines" of the personality. . . . Issues that may have been resolved long ago can be re-energized and re-emerge as a problem. Psychotherapy is a means to weather the emotional storm, reconnect with others, and re-establish confidence and a strong sense of personal identity. Another important goal of treatment would be helping these individuals find a sense of meaning or purpose in life based on their current life situation. The victim's efforts to deny or hide deficits and the tendency to withdraw are two major factors working against the effectiveness of therapy and must be addressed.

In this study, we have seen the conflicts that the head injured individual faces in relating to family and the problems that this generates. The inclusion of the family unit in the therapeutic process is important from a holistic viewpoint. Studies, such as that of Brooks and McKinlay (1983), have shown a direct relationship between the degree of emotional and behavioral disruption that the victims experience and the emotional and behavioral disruption found in the family. The family must be considered not only for the stress it is undergoing, and the additional stress it can create, but also for the support it can provide. According to Mauss-Clum and Ryan (1981) patients with strong family support progressed further that those without support.

It appears likely that many of the dominant components of the experience of closed head injury may also be applicable to other neurological syndromes. Multiple sclerosis, Parkinson's disease, and strokes are a few disorders where similar symptomatology may lead to the emotionally charged and constant struggle to retain an identity where issues of being changed, loss of emotional equilibrium, decreased awareness, fear of the future, dependent relationships, and feelings of alienation and disconnection are daily reminders of uncertainty, disability and loss of self-esteem. (Paskiewicz, 1988, pp. 100-103) [Reprinted by permission of the author]

Schneider's Study of the Mother-Daughter Relationship

In this section of a phenomenological study, the investigator, having become an expert on the topic, reflects on and provides ideas and recommendations and offers implications and outcomes that contribute to individual, societal, and family life, and to one's profession. Schneider's

(1987) study of the mother-daughter relationship offers an exemplary portrayal of implications and outcomes aimed at promoting greater understanding of the processes involved in the unfolding mother-daughter relationship from dependence to mutuality and autonomy. Knowledge of the processes and developmental shifts contributes to self-affirmation of mother and daughter and promotes positive and healthy interactions.

The excerpt that follows briefly outlines the implications of her data suggested by knowledge derived from the developmental phases of the mother-daughter relationship.

The insights and understandings that emerge as a result of this study have tremendous potential value for utilization on a personal and professional as well as societal level.

Specifically, the study points to the following outcomes and implications:

(1) That women are strongly seeking to understand their lives as impacted by the relationship with their daughters and to find a support system to give them the courage and strength to live through the dark times and to rejoice in the happy and loving moments.

(2) That there is a developmental agenda for both mother and daughter in terms of identity formation and re-definition of self. It is clear from my participants' experiences that their increased awareness of the dynamics associated with each phase of the mother-daughter process reduced their feelings of helplessness and provided a grounding and validation of their own effectiveness as mothers and as women.

(3) That knowledge is power and that understanding opens up the possibility for change.

(4) That the process takes a certain amount of time and that time is essential to the process.

(5) A perspectival view helps women to understand that each phase of the process has unique features. The beginning is marked by the tension of holding on, the middle is alive with struggle, and the passage of time allows for the growing recognition on the part of the mother that she could let go without losing the relationship.

(6) Regardless of the quality and/or quantity of support and intervention from the father, mothers perceive themselves to have primary responsibility to their adolescent daughter's physical as well as emotional well being. This finding implies a correlation to the polar feeling states that emerge as women attempt to integrate careers, personal interests, and other involvements that take time and attention away from the home. Additionally, this dimension becomes an arena of conflicts between husband and wife during stressful periods of the mother-daughter relationship.

This latter finding has several clinical applications in that it would be helpful to clarify role definitions and expectations, as well as to create openings for ongoing communication between the parents, enabling them to support one another and share their individual strengths in a mutually beneficial way.

The implications for society point to the continuation of efforts to heighten public awareness, raise the public conscience, and generate greater understanding of women's feelings, as well as greater opportunities for men to share in parenting.

(7) That the societal moves that have raised the social consciousness regarding women's rights and that have created openings and possibilities for women are often experienced with ambivalence. It appears that women feel torn between the allure of finding expression outside the home and the desire to parent in a way that is consistent with their valuing of physical and emotional availability to their offspring. The findings in this area imply a need to be aware of the polarities between the way society currently portrays the modern woman, and what women express as lived experiences. Additionally, it appears that women are seeking to find a balance in this area of their lives; the data point to several possibilities for societal intervention in the creation of academic and career opportunities with enough flexibility to allow women to use their talents and skills while parenting in a way that is congruent with their beliefs and values.

(8) While it appears that women are struggling to find a balance between parenting and having careers outside the home, they, in fact, maintain that career and academic or other personal interests are enhancing of the mother-daughter relationship as a whole. Primarily, women correlate careers and other interests with personal growth, greater feelings of competency, and a general sense of self-esteem, all utilized as a source of strength and succor in responding to many of the demands of the mother-daughter relationship. Additionally, women who are involved and committed to interests outside the home appear to experience separation with less trauma than their counterparts who are more deeply rooted in the struggle for identity formation. This finding adds credence to the need for opportunities for women to participate in the world outside the home and further address the need for society to explore options that support women's search for authentic expression in a variety of ways.

(9) Finally, addressing the relevance of the process also has implications for society, especially in terms of the methods that a society utilizes to conduct scientific research and the regard that science has for the truth of self-search and self-disclosure of the constituents of experience. In this context, it is useful to offer one more example of knowledge and understanding gained through a process that is congruent with the inherent dignity of the experiencing person, and the right of persons to be heard and believed. . . .

On a personal level, the inception, execution, and completion of this research study has had a profound impact on my life and contributed immeasurably to my own growth and development. Having had the privilege of hearing from and communicating with women as they share their experience of the mother-daughter relationship has given me a sense of affirmation and validation for what I have already experienced, as well as support and courage to move forward toward an exciting future. For me, there was tremendous comfort in hearing from women who have been where I have been, and felt as I have, as well as from those who are further along in the process, who have given me a glimpse of what is to come. In moving through the study, I was able to integrate my learnings and gain a perspective of the whole.

While I have gained insights and understandings of a cognitive nature, I also recognize a change that is intra-psychic, and speaks to an internal shift, one that reflects the wholeness of my own learning.

Specifically, I have come to realize that the experience of the mother-daughter relationship during the daughter's adolescent years is connected to a very real, tangible process that can be examined and understood, and that it has certain parameters and structures that can be utilized for support and guidance. Additionally, I now understand that the fears and tensions that mark the beginning phase are not pathological, that the struggles re-cement a new bonding, and that ultimately love holds through time and space.

As my learnings have impacted my personal growth, I have also utilized content and process information from this study in my work as a psychologist, and find great reward in sharing these findings with women who are involved in this process. Further, I feel tremendous pride and pleasure in developing and carrying out a research study that is congruent with my beliefs and values about science and humanity. (Schneider, 1987, pp. 107-114) [Reprinted by permission of the author]

ENDING PHASE OF PHENOMENOLOGICAL PROJECT

Schneider's Investigation of the Mother-Daughter Relationship

I have selected another section of Schneider's (1987) study of the mother-daughter relationship as a fine example of how a phenomenological researcher brings the research to a close. Schneider used the invitation of the closing of her research to present her professional and personal views and the strengths and inspirations that she derived from staying "in touch with the wholeness of an experience, with its essence . . . thereby allowing the light of unity and love to illuminate periods of darkness, to remind me of the changing and unfolding nature of life as process, and the forever regenerating sources of personal power" (p. 118).

In bringing my study of the mother-daughter relationship to a close, it is appropriate to consider the findings in light of what is already known. This study has reviewed the existing literature as a means of positioning the research and of validating the existence of a need. Having completed a comprehensive search and scrutiny of the information relevant to this topic and having compared the findings of my own investigation to those in the literature review, I believe that the comprehensive textural and structural descriptions of mother-daughter relationships that were derived from my data add unique and significant portrayals to existing knowledge.

Specifically, this study differs from others in its methods and procedures, allowing me to come to an understanding of meanings, values, and essences that describe the mother-daughter relationship during the adolescent years. Additionally, this study addresses the wholeness of the experience, encompassing psychological, sociological, biological, as well as spiritual dimensions.

This study, unlike prior research, did not seek to offer advice or prescribe behavior, but rather to suggest openings and possibilities for awareness, insight, and action that are inherent in the self-search and self reports of my participants.

Further, while certain themes and issues regarding separation and identity formation can be gleaned from existing literature, no previous study brings together the situational with the experiential, and synthesizes the experience in a way that reflects the totality and wholeness of a critical human experience.

A single study in the prior research stands out as a qualitative investigation of the parenting experience. While I found *Ourselves and Our Children* (Boston Women's Health Book Collective, 1978) to be the closest manifestation of a descriptive depiction of this experience, it nevertheless fails to provide an integration of the core themes, or a unity of past, present and future. I believe that my study extends the descriptive analysis of the mother-adolescent daughter relationship, explicates the wholeness of the experience, is grounded in a philosophy that is consistent with its purposes and values, and is appropriate to the question that it seeks to clarify and explicate.

My research presents a descriptive process, depicting the dynamics of each phase, and chronicling the movements from holding on to letting go. Following the study to its conclusion further differentiates it from others by pointing to the polarities between the rootedness of the holding on phase to the soaring flights of letting go.

As I draw a curtain on the final act of this presentation, I revel in the knowledge that I have participated in a never-ending process. While this particular investigation has come to its conclusion in the conventional sense, the insights and understandings I have gained will influence my way of being and will remain with me forever.

The lessons I have learned in this process are primarily about the process of life itself, and about the possibilities for change that emerge when persons adhere to perspectives based on commitment, wholeness, and caring. Further, as in the data, I have come to a personal sense of relationship to my daughter, one that is very satisfying; even as my life continues to unfold and as I continue to grow and learn new things in that relationship I am finding within myself something basic and integral to live by, something that will strengthen me and offer new directions for life's challenges.

This journey was conceived in the heart of the searcher, the process born in response to a beckoning call, the conclusion grew out of vivid descriptions of experience that make scientific research possible and practical knowledge a reality. (Schneider, 1987, pp. 116-119) [Reprinted by permission of the author]

CREATING THE RESEARCH MANUSCRIPT

As a guide to developing a manuscript that effectively organizes and presents a phenomenological study, in Appendix D I offer a detailed outline on how to construct the research manuscript. The outline includes guides to developing an Introduction and Statement of Topic and Outline, conducting and organizing a Review of Relevant Literature, developing and presenting the Conceptual Framework of the Transcendental Phenomenological Model, including a section on Methodology and Ways of Presenting the Data, and a final section on the Summary, Implications, and Outcomes of the Study.

CONCLUDING COMMENTS

My own applications of the transcendental phenomenological model presented in this volume have been a consistently rewarding experience, bringing a new kind of passionate involvement into my world and a way of actively participating in the lives of others, a way of witnessing and lifting out the qualities, constituents, and significant horizons of experience. I feel certain that I will continue to make modifications and refinements of the model but I am also convinced that as it stands it offers a valuable resource, a way of knowledge and discovery of the meanings and essences of human experience. It offers processes and methods that require effective listening and hearing, seeing things as they appear and as they are, not judging them, learning to describe experience rather than explain or analyze it, focusing on a core question and exploring in depth the everyday constituents of human experiences.

The transcendental phenomenological model offers a way of interrelating subjective and objective factors and conditions, a way of utilizing description, reflection, and imagination in arriving at an understanding of what is, in seeing the conditions through which what is comes to be, and in utilizing a process that in its very application opens possibilities for awareness, knowledge, and action.

REFERENCES

Alpern, N. (1984). Men and menstruation: A phenomenological investigation of men's experience of menstruation. (Doctoral dissertation, Union for Experimenting Colleges and Universities, 1983). *Dissertation Abstracts International, 44,* 2883B.

Bartz, C. (1988). An exploratory study of the coronary artery bypass graft experience. *Heart & Lung, 17*(2), 179-183.

Beckie, T. (1989). A supportive-educative telephone program: Impact on knowledge and anxiety after coronary artery bypass graft surgery. *Heart & Lung, 18*(1), 46-55.

Ben-Yishay, Y., & Diller, L. (1983a). Cognitive defects. In M. Rosenthal, E. R. Griffith, M. R. Bond, J. D. Miller (Eds.), *Rehabilitation of the head injured adult* (pp. 167-184). Philadelphia: F. A. Davis.

Ben-Yishay, Y., & Diller, L. (1983b). In M. Rosenthal, E. R. Griffith, M. R. Bond, J. D. Miller (Eds.), *Rehabilitation of the head injured adult* (pp. 367-379). Philadelphia: F. A. Davis.

Boston Women's Health Book Collective. (1978). *Ourselves and our children: A book by and for parents.* New York: Random House.

Brooks, D. N., & McKinlay, W. (1983). Personality and behavioral change after severe blunt head injury—A relative's view. *Journal of Neurology, Neurosurgery and Psychiatry, 46,* 336-344.

Cupples, S. A. (1991). Effects of timing and reinforcement of preoperative education on knowledge and recovery of patients having coronary artery bypass graft surgery. *Heart & Lung, 20*(6), 654-660.

Diller, L., & Gordon, W. A. (1981). Rehabilitation and clinical neuropsychology. In S. B. Filskov & T. J. Boll (Eds.), *Handbook of clinical neuropsychology* (pp. 702-733). New York: John Wiley.

Dikmen, S., & Reitan, R. M. (1977). Emotional sequelae of head injury. *Annals of Neurology, 2,* 492-494.

Dracup, K., Moser, D. K., Marseden, C., Taylor, S. E., & Guzy, P. M. (1991). Effects of a multidimensional cardiopulmonary rehabilitation program on psychosocial function. *American Journal of Cardiology, 68*(1), 31-34.

Gilliss, C. L. (1984). Reducing family stress during and after coronary artery bypass surgery, *19*(1), 103-111.

Goldschmidt, T., Brooks, N., Sethia, B., Wheatly, D. J., & Bond, M. (1984). Coronary artery bypass surgery—Impact upon a patient's wife—A pilot study. *Thoracic Cardiovascular Surgery, 32*(6), 337-340.

Langeluddecke, P., Tennant, C., Fulcher, G., Bariad, D., & Hughes, C. (1989). Coronary artery bypass surgery—Impact upon the patient's spouse, *33*(2), 155-159.

Mauss-Clum, N., & Ryan, M. (1981). Brain injury and the family. *Journal of Neuropsychological Nursing, 13*(4), 165-169.

Mulgan, R., & Logan, R. L. (1990). The coronary bypass waiting list: A social evaluation. *New Zealand Medical Journal, 103*(895), 371-372.

Paskiewicz, P. (1988). The experience of a traumatic closed head injury: A phenomenological study. (Doctoral dissertation, Union for Experimenting Colleges and Universities, 1987). *Dissertation Abstracts International, 49,* 919B.

Penckofer, S., & Holm, K. (1987). Hopes and fears after coronary artery bypass surgery. *Progressive Cardiovascular Nursing, 2*(4), 139-146.

Radley, A., & Green, R. (1986). Bearing illness: Study of couples where husbands await coronary graft surgery. *Social Science Medicine, 18*(6), 622-626.

Saudia, T. L., Kinney, M. R., Brown, K. C., & Young-Ward, L. (1991). Health locus of control and helpfulness of prayer. *Heart & Lung, 20*(1), 60-65.

Schmidt, L. (1992). *The shadow as a Jungian archetype.* Unpublished doctoral dissertation, The Union Institute, Cincinnati, OH.

Schneider, E. (1987). The mother's experience of the mother-daughter relationship during the daughter's adolescent years. (Doctoral dissertation, The Union Graduate School, 1986). *Dissertation Abstracts International, 48,* 2109B.

Stratman, C. (1990). The experience of personal power for women. (Doctoral dissertation, The Union Institute, 1989). *Dissertation Abstracts International, 50,* 5896B.

Thurer, S., Levine, F., & Thurer, R. (1980). The psychodynamic impact of coronary bypass surgery. *International Journal of Psychiatry Medicine, 10*(3), 273-290.

Trumbull, M. (1993). The experience of undergoing coronary artery bypass surgery: A phenomenological investigation. (Doctoral dissertation, The Union Institute, 1993). *Dissertation Abstracts International, 54,* 1115B.

APPENDIX A

Letter to Co-Researchers

Date _____

Dear _____,

Thank you for your interest in my dissertation research on the experience of coronary artery bypass surgery. I value the unique contribution that you can make to my study and I am excited about the possibility of your participation in it. The purpose of this letter is to reiterate some of the things we have already discussed and to secure your signature on the participation-release form that you will find attached.

The research model I am using is a qualitative one through which I am seeking comprehensive depictions or descriptions of your experience. In this way I hope to illuminate or answer my question: "What is the experience of undergoing coronary artery bypass surgery?"

Through your participation as a co-researcher, I hope to understand the essence of coronary artery bypass surgery as it reveals itself in your experience. You will be asked to recall specific episodes, situations, or events that you experienced in undergoing coronary artery bypass surgery. I am seeking vivid, accurate, and comprehensive portrayals of what these experiences were like for you: your thoughts, feelings, and behaviors, as well as situations, events, places, and people connected with your experience.

I value your participation and thank you for the commitment of time, energy, and effort. If you have any further questions before signing the release form or if there is a problem with the date and time of our meeting, I can be reached at [telephone number].

With warm regards,

Mike Trumbull

Participant Release Agreement

I agree to participate in a research study of "What is the experience of undergoing coronary artery bypass surgery?" I understand the purpose and nature of this study and I am participating voluntarily. I grant permission for the data to be used in the process of completing a Ph.D. degree, including a dissertation and any other future publication. I understand that a brief synopsis of each participant, including myself, will be used and will include the following information: first name, marital status, number of children, number of grandchildren, occupation, factors/symptoms that lead to seeing a cardiologist, time between tests and recommendation to have bypass, and the actual surgery, date of the bypass, number of bypasses, age at the time of bypass, and any other pertinent information that will help the reader come to know and recall each participant. I grant permission for the above personal information to be used. I agree to meet at the following location _____ on the following date _____ at _____ for an initial interview of 1 to 2 hours. If necessary, I will be available at a mutually agreed upon time and place for an additional 1 to 1½ hour interview. I also grant permission to tape-recording of the interview(s).

_____   _____
Research Participant/Date   Primary Researcher/Date

APPENDIX B

Thank You Letter to Co-Researchers

Date _____

Dear _____,

Thank you for meeting with me in an extended interview and sharing your bypass experience. I appreciate your willingness to share your unique and personal thoughts, feelings, events, and situations. I have enclosed a transcript of your interview. Would you please review the entire document? Be sure to ask yourself if this interview has fully captured your experience of bypass surgery. After reviewing the transcript of the interview, you may realize that an important experience(s) was neglected. Please feel free to add comments, with the enclosed red pen, that would further elaborate your experience(s), or if you prefer we can arrange to meet again and tape record your additions or corrections. Please do not edit for grammatical corrections. The way you told your story is what is critical.

When you have reviewed the verbatim transcript and have had an opportunity to make changes and additions, please return the transcript in the stamped, addressed envelope.

I have greatly valued your participation in this research study and your willingness to share your experience. If you have any questions or concerns, do not hesitate to call me.

With warm regards,

Mike Trumbull

APPENDIX C

Outline Summary of the Phenomenological Model

Processes:

Epoche: Setting aside prejudgments and opening the research interview with an unbiased, receptive presence

Phenomenological Reduction

  Bracketing the Topic or Question

  Horizonalization: Every statement has equal value

  Delimited Horizons or Meanings: Horizons that stand out as invariant qualities of the experience

  Invariant Qualities and Themes: Nonrepetitive, nonoverlapping constituents clustered into themes

  Individual Textural Descriptions: An integration, descriptively, of the invariant textural constituents and themes of each research participant

  Composite Textural Description: An integration of all of the individual textural descriptions into a group or universal textural description

Imaginative Variation

  Vary Possible Meanings

  Vary Perspectives of the Phenomenon: From different vantage points, such as opposite meanings and various roles

Free Fantasy Variations: Consider freely the possible structural qualities or dynamics that evoke the textural qualities

Construct a list of structural qualities of the experience

Develop Structural Themes: Cluster the structural qualities into themes

Employ Universal Structures as Themes: Time, space, relationship to self, to others; bodily concerns, causal or intentional structures

Individual Structural Descriptions: For each co-researcher, integrate the structural qualities and themes into an individual structural description

Composite Structural Description: An integration of all of the individual structural descriptions into a group or universal structural description of the experience

Synthesis of Composite Textural and Composite Structural Descriptions

Intuitively-reflectively integrate the composite textural and composite structural descriptions to develop a synthesis of the meanings and essences of the phenomenon or experience

Methodology

Preparing to Collect Data

1. Formulate the question: Define terms of question

2. Conduct literature review and determine original nature of study

3. Develop criteria for selecting participants: Establish contract, obtain informed consent, insure confidentiality, agree to place and time commitments, and obtain permission to record and publish

4. Develop instructions and guiding questions or topics needed for the phenomenological research interview

Collecting Data

1. Engage in the Epoche process as a way of creating an atmosphere and rapport for conducting the interview

2. Bracket the question

3. Conduct the qualitative research interview to obtain descriptions of the experience. Consider:

   a. Informal interviewing

   b. Open-ended questions

   c. Topical-guided interview

Organizing, Analyzing, and Synthesizing Data

Follow modified van Kaam method or Stevick-Colaizzi-Keen method

Develop individual textural and structural descriptions; composite textural and composite structural descriptions, and a synthesis of textural and structural meanings and essences of the experience

Summary, Implications, and Outcomes

Summarize entire study

Relate study findings to and differentiate from findings of literature review

Relate study to possible future research and develop an outline for a future study

Relate study to personal outcomes

Relate study to professional outcomes

Relate study to social meanings and relevance

Offer closing comments: Researcher's future direction and goals

APPENDIX D

Creating the Research Manuscript

Chapter I. Introduction and Statement of Topic and Outline

Out of what autobiographical ground and experience did the topic emerge? What stands out (a few critical incidents) that creates a puzzlement, curiosity, passion to know? Does the topic have social implications and relevance? What new knowledge do you anticipate that would contribute to your profession? To you as a person and learner?

State your question. Define and elucidate its terms.

Chapter II. Review of the Relevant Literature

Include discussion of computer search, databases, descriptors, key words, years covered, summary of database printout lists. Also include summary and findings of "manual" and "library" search.

Organize literature review to include: *Introduction:* present clearly topic or theme of the review, give overview and discussion of methodological problems; *Methods:* describe what induced you to include study (criteria for selecting), how studies were conducted, *include a few examples; Themes:* organize studies into embracing themes and cluster the themes into patterns in presenting findings; *Summary and Conclusions:* summarize core findings relevant to your research, differentiate your investigation from prior research—including your question, model, methodology, data to be collected.

Chapter III. Conceptual Framework of Model

Develop conceptual framework of model; include theory, concepts, and processes that delineate the essentials of your research design.

Chapter IV. Methodology

Include methods and procedures developed in *preparing* to conduct the study, in *collecting* the data, and in *organizing, analyzing,* and *synthesizing* the data.

Chapter V. Presentation of Data

Include verbatim examples illustrating the collection of data and its analysis and synthesis. Include examples of horizonalization, horizons or meaning units, clustering of horizons into themes, individual textural descriptions, individual structural descriptions, the composite textural description, the composite structural description, and the synthesis of meanings and essences of the experience.

Chapter VI. Summary, Implications, and Outcomes

Summarize the study in brief, vivid terms from its inception to its final synthesis of data.

Now that your investigation has been completed, how, in fact, do your findings differ from findings presented in your literature review?

What future studies might you or others conduct as an outcome of your research? Develop at least one project in detail.

What limitations existed in your research methodology and findings?

What implications, if any, are relevant to society? To your profession? To education? To you as a learner and as a person?

Write a brief creative close that speaks to the essence of the study and its inspiration to you in terms of the value of the knowledge and future directions of your professional-personal life.

* Chapters III and IV might be combined as one chapter.

AUTHOR INDEX

185

SUBJECT INDEX

Aristotelian philosophy:
term "intention" in, 28

Books in Print, 112

Center for Humanistic Studies, 62

Dissertation Abstracts International, 112

Empirical Phenomenological Research,
1, 11-16, 21
aim of, 13
analysis methods of, 13
descriptive levels of, 13
target of, 14
Epoche process, 22, 26, 33-34, 38, 39,
41, 60, 61, 78, 85-90, 94, 96, 101,
116, 153, 180, 181
challenge of, 86
definition of, 85

difficulty of achieving, 87-89
receptiveness and, 89
reflective-meditation and, 89
versus Cartesian doubt, 85
ERIC, 112
Ethnography, 1-4, 8, 21
cultural description as result of, 2
example of, 3
strategies of, 2-3
values of, 3-4

Galileo, 48
Grounded Research Theory, 1, 4-7, 8, 21
labeling process of, 5-6
practices of, 5
tenets of, 5
ultimate aim of, 4

Hegel, G. W. F., 26
Hermeneutics, 1, 8-11, 21
analysis process of, 11
and hermeneutic circle, 10

ABOUT THE AUTHOR

Clark Moustakas is President of the Center for Humanistic Studies in Detroit and Senior Consultant and Core Faculty Member in Psychology at the Union Institute in Cincinnati. His development as a person and as a psychologist is reflected in his studies and publications grounded in psychological, philosophical, educational, and literary perspectives, values, and concepts that underlie, enrich, and deepen human discoveries, meanings, and experiences. His publications on loneliness, creativity and conformity, teaching and learning, psychotherapy, and qualitative research retain an interdisciplinary unity of mind and soul.

DATE DUE

MY 16 '04			
JY 22 '04			
Sept. 4 '04			
NO 12 '04			
JA 5 '05			
JA 02 '06			
AP 2 '06			
OC 30 '06			
JAN 02 2010			